i piccoli
di arsenale

Patrizia Fabbri

Palaces
of Florence

arsenale editrice

Patrizia Fabbri
PALACES OF FLORENCE

photographs
Stefano Giraldi

layout
Stefano Grandi

printing
EBS Editoriale Bortolazzi-Stei
Verona

first edition
May 2000

Arsenale Editrice srl
via Querini 100
30172 Venice Mestre
Italy

Arsenale Editrice © 2000

ISBN 88-7743-214-4

Contents

Introduction

It often happens that the genesis, history and development of a city are determined by the interaction between a series of environmental, social, architectural, economic and cultural factors. Some of the elements that come together to define the shape and form of an urban settlement might therefore offer a singular key, affording us a deeper reading of this type of analysis. One such element (and by no means a marginal one) is doubtless the palazzo, intended not so much, or not only, as an inhabitable space, but above all as the symbolic mirror of a social situation, a family's conditions and a public function. Florence in particular constitutes a truly remarkable example: it would by no means be excessive to state that, by looking at the palazzi, we could analyse the important phases in the city's more recent history, where by "recent" we intend the last 800 years or so – from the freedom offered by the comune to the Medici, from the Grand Duchy to the city's rise to capital of the newly-formed Kingdom of Italy, right up to the present, with the definitive affirmation of the Republic. Going beyond the theatrical and official façade of these elegant residences and penetrating their most intimate nature we can uncover ways of life, customs and traditions as they have changed over the centuries. The first thirteenth and fourteenth century palazzi, such as the overwhelmingly impressive Palazzo Feroni and Palazzo Davanzati, allow us to imagine a city life that was probably not always easy and quite often violent; the spectacular Medici palazzi, from Palazzo Medici Riccardi to Palazzo Pitti, open up the rooms where the events of a powerful dynasty took place. The great noble residences, from Palazzo Della Gherardesca to Palazzo Corsini, bear witness to the arrival of the Grand Duchy in the 16th century and how this changed the habits and needs of the local aristocracy, who were called to the Grand Duke's court and made to assume specific representational roles. Thus Florence, which has never lost its intricate medieval weave, which has always been proud of its own independence and wealthy mercantile activities, which has often assumed the role of absolute leader in the highest moments of the Italy's history, can still tell the story of its most representative families through its palazzi, each of which is distinctive in terms of its origins, conception, structure, architecture, ornamentation and function. These palazzi, in fact, tell the tale of the centuries-old evolution of the city itself.

The Public Palazzo

In the cities of the Middle Ages, the palazzo was not featured in the architecture of private homes. That is to say, there were no palazzi that belonged to individual families, however rich or influential a family might be. Powerful families tended to live in groups of houses that were adjacent to each other, interconnected, and grouped around a shared interior courtyard; these houses came to constitute independent city blocks. Features were added to make them safe from attack: towers were added, windows were made small and narrow, the houses rose high and sheer into the sky.

Palazzi, rather, were buildings erected to contain the magistracies and all the officials of government, in towns and cities that were very proud of their communal institutions and their ancient freedoms, which they identified with their palazzi. The palazzo, therefore, was a public building, the hub of political life.

Florence was no exception to this rule. The first palazzo built in Florence was the Palazzo del Capitano del Popolo (1255), later known as the Bargello in recognition of the sole official representative of the Commune, or city government, who had previously been obliged to make do with improvised lodgings and offices. The most prestigious palazzo was built just over thirty years later, on behalf of the Priori delle Arti, the heads of the various guilds; this Palazzo dei Priori was later named the Palazzo della Signoria. The Priori were representatives of powerful guilds. These guilds encompassed a good portion of the city's population, organized according to trade or craft. In time, they became arbiters of city life, and with the passing decades, they became, in practice, the single most influential magistracy in Florence. And so, when the decision was made to build an appropriate building to house them, the city turned to the most highly esteemed architect in Florence, a master builder of public works at the end of the thirteenth century, Arnolfo di Cambio. This pupil of Nicola Pisano was now past fifty, and had already completed outstanding and lovely buildings; at this time, he was engaged in the construction of the new cathedral, Santa Maria del Fiore.

Arnolfo planned a precise network of links and relationships in the context of a more general urban renewal. The cathedral and the Palazzo dei Priori would be symmetrically located at opposite ends of an axis (along a radius

connected to the ancient ring of the walled perimeter) constituted by Via dei Calzaiuoli. These two buildings would thus establish a monumental complex occupying the heart of the city, in which the two great authorities—church and state—were symbolically united. Each would be symbolized in a deftly managed interplay of volume and bulk: the two preeminent structures were the dome, on one side, and the tower, on the other.

But when Arnolfo began work on the Palazzo dei Priori, in 1298, he suddenly found himself fettered by limitations of space and foregone decisions, imposed by existing circumstances. The Florentine historian Giovanni Villani offers a clear account of it in his book, *Cronica Universale* (Book VIII, chapter XXVI).

First of all, he had to keep in mind that in the area selected for the construction of the new building had once stood the houses of the Uberti family. This family had been a leading force in the Ghibelline faction, outlawed when the opposing Guelphs finally and definitively triumphed. As was customary in such cases, all property of the Uberti family had been declared forfeit and confiscated; their buildings had been razed to the ground. Where those buildings had once stood, it was decreed that a plaza be built, and there was a total and inviolable prohibition against building on the plaza, lest the houses of the Uberti family be rebuilt. And that was not all. Not far away stood the church of San Piero Scheraggio, which, as a house of worship, could not be demolished.

Between these two locations stood the houses of the Foraboschi family, with the towering Torre della Vacca, which the city government hurriedly purchased. They were torn down, and in their place the new Palazzo dei Priori soon rose.

Constrained by these precise strictures, Arnolfo took the Torre della Vacca as a starting point; upon the foundations of this tower, he built the new Torre dei Priori, now known as the Torre di Arnolfo. At the base of this tower, Arnolfo built the majestic parallelepiped structure that constituted the original core of the building, surrounding a porticoed courtyard which was later renovated in the fifteenth century by Michelozzo. The true

< Palazzo Vecchio, Bronzino, *Stories of Moses* (ca. 1564)

facade of the building was originally the short side, facing north, with the portal placed appropriately at deadcentre. It was not until many decades later that the main entrance became the present one, on the side facing west, opening more directly onto the square as it finally took form, closed off by the Loggia dei Lanzi. Because it had not originally been designed as the main portal, it was asymmetrically located with respect to the new facade, as was the tower; and so it has remained to the present day.

In the construction of what was to become Florence's public palace *par excellence*, Arnolfo remained faithful to the typical features of medieval

Giorgio Vasari, *The Apotheosis of Cosimo*, 1560-1572

civil architecture: the tower, the courtyard with portico, and the vaulted hall on the ground floor, divided into two aisles. Directly corresponding to this hall, on the floor above, was the Sala del Consiglio. Originally one entered this hall by an exterior staircase, as was common.

Alongside these features of medieval civil architecture, however, Arnolfo added other elements that were taken directly from military architecture: the galleries of the eaves, merlons or parapets, and the tower itself, conceived as a defensive structure, completely solid, unbroken by windows; it was built to hold the bell, which rang to announce sessions of the Consiglio, or Council. The bell in question had previously hung in the church of San Piero Scheraggio, mentioned previously.

Arnolfo thus created a homogeneous structure with a well-defined identity, despite the variety of its component parts. This building rose majestically above the surrounding city; the tower stood about 317 feet tall, while the building itself stood about 141 feet at the uppermost gallery. Construction was definitively completed around 1330. The building survived revolutions and transitions of all sorts, from the Seigneury to the Grand Duchy, to the Kingdom, and finally to the modern-day Republic. Even now, seven centuries after its construction, Palazzo Vecchio houses the offices of the mayor of Florence and the city council.

Among the numerous institutional changes that affected the Palazzo della Signoria, one of the most significant was certainly the advent of the powerful Medici family at the helm of the state. This event was anything but traumatic or sudden; it was the result of a patient brick-by-brick process, characteristically concrete, as was to be expected from a family of merchants. It was the work of many different members of the Medici family. Certainly, a decisive contribution came from Cosimo, known as Cosimo the Elder, who was the son of Giovanni di Bicci, who can rightly be considered the founder of this family's fortunes. He had quickly understood that, in order to obtain a position of real power and preeminence in Florence, it was necessary to act with extreme discretion. There could be no ostentation of luxury and power. He would have to maneuver behind the scenes, manipulating the city's public life while making a show of respect

Palazzo Medici Riccardi, the two *fenestre inginocchiate* designed by Michelangelo

and devotion to the most important Republican institutions.

Cosimo transformed this intuition into a full-bodied political program; he never abandoned it, and he successfully handed it on to his own descendants. In fact, no Medici, until the fourth decade of the sixteenth century, ever held any public office—not even Lorenzo the Magnificent—even though the Medici family had held absolute power over Florence for nearly a century. Cosimo clung to this rule even when, around 1440, he decided that the time had come to build a palazzo worthy of his family's enormous ambitions. By this time other noble families had inaugurated the tradition of a large residence as a demonstration of financial might, and

Baccio Bandinelli, *Orpheus*, courtyard of Palazzo Medici Riccardi

as a safe and fortified haven for the immediate family. At first, at least in part from considerations of prestige, but also because of the architect's unquestioned talent, Cosimo turned to Filippo Brunelleschi, the architect who had, over the course of a few decades, altered the face of the city of Florence, turning it into a true Renaissance city. Brunelleschi produced a design and a wooden model of singular beauty: a building with a square floor plan, with nine windows on each face. According to Brunelleschi's plans, it would stand directly across from the church of San Lorenzo. This was an ambitious project, and the outlay would have been enor-

Palazzo Medici Riccardi, Frescoes painted by Luca Giordano for the baroque gallery >

following pages
Bartolomeo Ammannati, The façade of Palazzo Pitti, 1558-1570

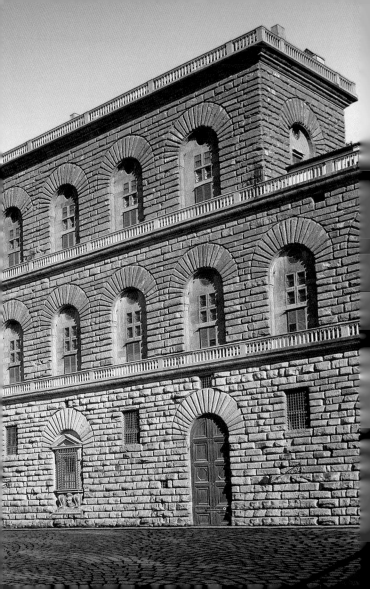

mous. Above all, it clashed with the discreet public image that Cosimo had chosen to adopt. Cosimo rejected the plan, more with a view to stifling envy than out of concern for the expense, as Vasari put it in his *Lives of the Most Eminent Italian Painters, Sculptors and Architects*. Instead, he turned to another architect who had also shown uncommon talent; in time, this architect was to prove to be the most skillful interpreter of the wishes and ambitions of Cosimo. It was Michelozzo.

Michelozzo, after initial contacts with Lorenzo Ghiberti and Donatello, had demonstrated a growing interest in Brunelleschi's approach. If Brunelleschi's work was sometimes rather abstract, Michelozzo moved it in the direction of the massive and powerful walls, stone, and facades in which the lines and surfaces were clearly marked and well defined.

Michelozzo had already worked for Cosimo once, when he renovated the convent of San Marco. On that occasion he had shown himself to be equal to the most demanding tasks.

And so, beginning in 1444, construction was undertaken of the Palazzo Medici of Via Larga (now Via Cavour). The architecture still maintains the typically medieval concept of the corner view as the fundamental perspective, with an innovative approach and original development of the volumes. The palazzo, in its original version had a main facade that overlooked Via Larga, with ten vertical bays of windows and three portals. (In the second half of the seventeenth century, the Riccardi family, which had purchased the building from the Medici in 1659—hence the modern name of Palazzo Medici Riccardi—enlarged it considerably, which resulted in the destruction of all the various annexes—stables, storehouses, kitchens—and the elimination of the carriage gateway).

The sheer upward thrust appeared to be in sharp contrast with the massive jutting cornice, intentionally designed to heighten the impression of stern power created by the gradated rustication along the three stories. In order to reinforce further the idea of a fortress-palazzo, a safe haven rather than an elegant residence, it was decided not to provide the ground floor—traditionally devoted to facilities (kitchen and bathroom) rather than living quarters—with windows. Windows were only added in the sixteenth century; they were designed by none other than Michelangelo, and are markedly different from the centred twin-light mullioned win-

dows that make such an elegant and lovely display on the second and third floors. Without a doubt, one of Michelozzo's finest creations is the courtyard of the palazzo, conceived in a transitional step between the convent cloister and the medieval courtyard. It has a lovely, ground-floor columned atrium, and an exquisite thirdfloor gallery with an Ionic colonnade. Of particular note is the painstaking decoration of the architrave that runs around the entire courtyard. This courtyard was soon taken as a model for many palazzo courtyards built after the middle of the fifteenth century. Also worthy of note is the small enclosed garden, meant to be used by the family alone, and still quite in keeping with the medieval atmosphere. The arrangement of the interior, on the other hand, is much more modern; the rooms are connected one to another along

The Boboli Gardens and, *on the right*, one the statue, the *Bacchino*

straight axes, so that each wing constitutes a self-contained apartment comprising living room, bedchamber, antechamber, and study. Cosimo was especially fond of the apartment overlooking the garden, while Lorenzo the Magnificent chose to live in the apartment overlooking Via Larga because it was directly connected to the principal receiving hall and the splendid chapel that had been designed by Michelozzo and decorated by Benozzo Gozzoli.

Palazzo Medici remained the urban residence of Florence's "reigning" family until 1540, which is to say, as long as it appeared advisable to adhere to Cosimo's avowed policy of separating the Medici's image as a private family from any public office. In 1537, however, another Cosimo, a grand-nephew, was officially declared duke and ruler of Florence. From that moment onward all caution appeared superfluous, and it became advisable, indeed, that the Medici family should move into the palazzo that had become symbolic of power in Florence, the Palazzo della Signoria, as Palazzo Vecchio was called in that period. Palazzo Medici was destined to be the home of the cadets and widows of the dynasty; in time it was sold to the Riccardi family, as explained above. All the same, because of the elegance of Palazzo Medici, because of its prestige—reflected in the name of its owners—and because of its long-standing role in the context of Florentine social life, it never lost its status as the model for most private homes in the fifteenth and sixteenth centuries. Many who had built homes in that period openly admitted that they wished their homes to rival Palazzo Medici in dignity. Today, the Florence Prefecture occupies the building; in the section added later by the Riccardi is the Biblioteca Riccardiana, a highly respected library.

When Grand Duke Cosimo moved into Palazzo della Signoria, he was newly married to Eleonora of Toledo, the young daughter of the Viceroy of Naples. For the duke and duchess it was quite a simple matter to settle into those sections of the palazzo that are still known as the *Appartamenti di Cosimo* and the *Appartamenti di Eleonora*. Before long, the marriage proved to be an extraordinarily prolific one Eleonora gave birth, one after the other, to Maria, Francesco, Isabella, Giovanni, Lucrezia, Anna, Pedricco, Garzia, Ferdinando, and Pietro. Palazzo della Signoria, which had most certainly not been designed to accommodate a family, much less

29

a large and growing family, soon proved inadequate. Cosimo began to look around for a new home. The home he sought was to have two qualities—it should be large enough to accommodate his numerous offspring, and it should not be too far away from the heart of political power in Florence, which in any case remained the Palazzo della Signoria.

His choice was the large house built by Luca Pitti, on the Colle di Boboli, in Oltrarno. Eleonora purchased it in 1549 for the price of 10,000 florins. Oddly enough, this great palazzo maintained the name of its first owner over the centuries, even though he had inhabited it only briefly, and despite the fact that for centuries it would be the residence of the grand-ducal family, and—after the unification of Italy—a royal palace. It is still known as Palazzo Pitti. Luca Pitti was an exceedingly wealthy merchant and a rival of the Medici family.

Shortly before 1450, Pitti asked Filippo Brunelleschi to build a new mansion for him. This home was to be lovelier than any other in Florence; it was to have windows larger than the portal of Palazzo Medici on Via Larga. The location of the new palazzo was quite unusual, distant from the centre of Florence and from the streets where the leading families generally built their homes. It was to overlook the surrounding countryside, not far from the Porta Romana. Brunelleschi completed his plans for the new palazzo in 1446, just before his death. The palazzo was built to his design. Many homes were confiscated and demolished in order to make room for the new *piazza*, or square, the first to lie before a private palazzo. Palazzo Pitti was built upon an exceptionally strong rock foundation, capable of supporting so large and weighty a building. Brunelleschi conceived the central wing as a simple, grand structure, three stories tall, with a progressively (floor-by-floor) smoother rustication. Facing the square were three portals and a series of windows that were identical to the portals (this last was quite a new concept). Moreover, the three central arches of the second floor were left open, creating the usual loggia, while there was a corresponding gallery in the rear facade, overlooking the countryside. On the whole, there is a clear impression of a building

preceeding pages and on the right
Sala III and Sala IV of the Museo degli Argenti (treasure chamber)

meant to be viewed from the front—an impression emphasized by the presence of the *piazza*—so that the emphasis was more on the layout of the surfaces and less on the creation of volumes. In the rear, because of the slope of the hill, the second story was level with the garden behind it. This, then, was a proud and impressive home, and a highly original piece of architecture. Work was interrupted in 1465, however, when the Pitti family fell into financial ruin. As soon as Cosimo and Eleonora purchased it, work resumed Bartolomeo Ammannati was hired to enlarge the exterior and interior of the palazzo. He had the necessary stone quarried from the courtyard itself, and from the garden. Construction continued until 1570, and the original design by Brunelleschi was respected.

In the meantime, Niccolò Pericoli, known as the Tribolo, was overseeing work on the gardens, which—with the later work done under Buontalenti and Alfonso Parigi—acquired the appearance that was to make the Boboli Gardens famous throughout the world. In the centuries that followed, the facade was further enlarged, first by Giulio Parigi (1620) and later by his son Alfonso Parigi (1640). The two side wings were added between 1764 and 1783, according to plans by Giuseppe Ruggieri.

As early as 1565, and in just six months' time, Cosimo de' Medici attained one of his most pressing requirements. Giorgio Vasari had designed and built a monumental corridor that ran across the Arno, directly connecting Cosimo's apartments in the Palazzo della Signoria with the grand-ducal home of Palazzo Pitti. Thus, the centre of political power and the private residence, though distant from one another, were united, symbolically underscoring the fact that Florence was ruled, irrevocably and permanently, by the Medici. Florence now had a third palazzo, and a garden that was a place for official reception and entertaining—a garden that was to become a model for many later gardens.

Nowadays, the palazzo houses the Museo degli Argenti, the Galleria Palatina, and the Galleria di Arte Moderna.

The portrait of Lorenzo the Magnificent painted in one of the chamber of the Museo degli Argenti

Guelphs and Ghibellines, and further degenerating into in-fighting between the two Guelph factions of the Whites (Bianchi) and the Blacks (Neri). During this period it was of special importance, especially for the most prominent families, to build a secure home. As a result, tower-houses were built, along with the stout fortified palazzi that looked like the strongholds that they in fact were. One of the chosen areas for these palazzi was the bank of the river Arno. Here the buildings could occupy a dominant position that was therefore easily defended; at the same time, if located near a bridge-head, the occupants could enjoy total control of a strategic point of communications.

Near one of these bridges, the Ponte a Santa Trinita, along the Borgo Santi Apostoli, the wealthy Spini family had most of its homes and real estate (the family was a leading presence in Florence as early as the thirteenth century). Members of the Arte del Cambio (Guild of the Moneychangers), the Spini family, through the family company, was for many years the banker for the pope, entitled to collect the tithes in Germany, Poland, Hungary, and Bohemia, and to make that income pay dividends. Many of them were also distinguished in public office in Florence; one of the leading members of the family was Geri, who served at the end of the thirteenth century as lieutenant general under King Roberto of Naples, and ambassador to the Holy See under Pope Boniface VIII; he had also fought valiantly for Florence at the great battle of Campaldino. In fact, Messer Geri degli Spini, who was a successful merchant with a considerable fortune, decided to take advantage of the disastrous flood of 1299—which had damaged many of the houses he owned along the Lungarno—to convert them into the stern and impressive palazzo-fortress we know today. For the thirteenth century, this was quite a large building. From the planning stages—some say it was designed by Geri degli Spini; others believe the architect was Lapo Tedesco—the palazzo was split into two sections, to be used by the two branches of the family.

The wing that overlooked the Piazza Santa Trinita was inherited by the descendants of Geri degli Spini, who lived there until 1651, the year in which another Geri degli Spini, the son of Cristofano degli Spini, died without heirs. About this Geri degli Spini we know that when he inherited the building, the single facade covered three separate residences, the result of the combination of original thirteenth-century houses.

Between 1606 and 1611 this latter-day Geri degli Spini arranged to uni-

fy the various residential units. He then hired Bernardino Poccetti to decorate the rooms with series of frescoes. When this branch of the Spini family died out, their wing of the palazzo had a series of new owners first Niccolò Guasconi, then Simone da Bagnano (whose family undertook a great many projects to improve the interior, moving the elegant little chapel to its present location). On the exterior, they gave the facade an odd Baroque appearance, with new pediments and decorations. Finally, in 1768 another wealthy merchant, the marchese Francesco Antonio Feroni purchased it. In the meantime, the portion of the palazzo that overlooked the Arno—which had remained the property of the other branch of the Spini family—was transferred by marriage to the Del Tovaglia family by Camilla, the sole heir of Guglielmo di Jacopo degli Spini, in 1686. From that family the palazzo was passed to the Pitti family and then, in 1807, it was purchased by Francesco Feroni. By the nineteenth century, then, the palazzo had once again become the property of a single family, and it took their name. In 1834 the entire building became the property of another wealthy family, the Homberts. They converted it into an elegant and prestigious hotel. Its luxurious homes received illustrious guests such as Metternich and Tsar Alexander of Russia. But the palazzo did not remain a hotel for long. In 1846 the city government of Florence purchased it for 34,500 *scudi* (old units of Italian currency), and converted it into city hall. The building erected by Geri degli Spini remained the office building of Florence's city administration for twenty years, until Florence lost its short-lived standing as capital of Italy, and was replaced by Rome. Palazzo Feroni returned to obscurity and was used for a number of different functions. New renovations were undertaken, this time to restore its original appearance, with the elimination of superstructures that had been added to the facade by the da Bagnano family. On January 15, 1881, in the context of an agreement to settle the city's debts, Florence deeded the palazzo—valued at 1,252,000 lire—to the Cassa di Risparmio di Firenze, a banking institution. The Cassa di Risparmio di Firenze in turn sold it to a certain Ruggero Casardi. Since that time, Palazzo Feroni has increasingly become a commercial building, containing the offices of leading companies, which have successfully settled into the old edifice, fully respecting its remarkable history.

Palazzo Malenchini Alberti
Via dei Benci 1

The entire area between Via dei Benci and Piazza Santa Croce was once occupied by the homes of the Alberti family. Many of these houses were demolished by enraged Ghibellines following their victory at the battle of Montaperti, though the ancient tower at the corner of Borgo Santa Croce remains standing. It was probably as a response to these events that the Alberti family began to purchase land, still on Via dei Benci, but toward the Lungarno, on a line with the Ponte alle Grazie. At that time the palazzo was hemmed in by a welter of densely packed buildings. As for the

Alberti family, they clearly exerted considerable influence over every aspect of life in this quarter of Florence. They provided constant support for the construction of the church of Santa Croce, and Jacopo Alberti made a commitment to erect an oratory on the bridge, in honour of the Madonna delle Grazie (Our Lady of Grace). The bridge received its present name—Ponte alle Grazie—in recognition.

Things did not even change very much when the Alberti family was sentenced to exile, due to their rivalry with the triumphant faction of the Albizzi. The Alberti were back in Florence by 1434, with the favour of the Medici, and thereafter their star never really dimmed.

As for their residence on Via dei Benci, at the corner with the Lungarno,

it was not until the eighteenth century that it could properly be described as a palazzo. It was in fact Giovan Vincenzio Alberti who arranged to unify the facade and the interior of the building (1760-1763). Giovan Vincenzio's son, Leon Battista, was the last of the Alberti. When he died in 1836, he left the entire estate to a niece, a member of the Mori Ubaldini family. In order to respect a clause in the will that required that the Alberti name be perpetuated, the inheritors became the Alberti Mori Ubaldini family. The new owners immediately set about a number of major renovations: they hired the architect Vittorio Bellini to undertake improvements to the interior of the palazzo and in the garden. Bellini built a *tepidarium* (a warm sitting-room in the ancient Roman baths) as well as an elevation with neoclassical columns that contains the garden near the Lungarno.

As for the facade, the architect O. Rezzi successfully endowed it with a new, quattrocento-style appearance in 1849. The new facade was spare and elegant, in keeping with the origins of the palazzo itself. Shortly thereafter, however, the count Arturo Alberti Mori Ubaldini found himself unable to meet his mounting debts. He was forced to sell the family palazzo to another branch of the Alberti family, the Alberti del Giudice. This branch of the family had been residents of France for some time, and had been made dukes of Chaulnes, Luynes, and Chevreuse. The Alberti del Giudice remained in Florence for only about twenty years. Thus, at the end of the nineteenth century, their palazzo became the property of the marchese Luigi Malenchini, a descendant of the famous Vincenzo Malenchini; for the latter's distinguished service during the Italian Risorgimento, he had been made a Senator of the Kingdom of Italy. The palazzo's new owners were profoundly affected by two calamitous events during the twentieth century, each of which threatened the structural integrity of the palazzo. First was the destruction of the bridges over the river Arno by the Germans in 1944. Palazzo Malenchini, on a line with the Ponte alle Grazie, was hit directly by the blast. The second threat was the great flood of the Arno in 1966, when the silty floodwaters swept through the ground floor of the palazzo and devastated the garden and its exotic plants. The garden, the ground floor, and the entire palazzo have since been entirely restored, and the Marchesi Malenchini are still the owners of this palazzo.

Palazzo Davanzati
Via Porta Rossa

On the centrally located Via Porta Rossa, midway between the imposing Palazzo Strozzi and the Arno, stands a tall, impressive building. Because of its remarkable architecture and structural characteristics, paradoxically enough, this building has been largely overlooked through the centuries. Its steep narrow staircases; its dark, stern rooms, some more than one story in height; and even the outer structure's sheer vertical height— all these features were sharply at odds with the ideas of comfort and refinement that developed over the ensuing centuries. This building is Palazzo Davanzati, erected in the fourteenth century by the powerful Davizzi family. A number of members of this family are depicted in the capitals of the columns in the courtyard, and visitors can still admire their features. In 1516, the Davizzi family sold their home to their wealthy neighbours, the Bartolini Salimbeni family; they in turn sold it to Bernardo Davanzati in 1578. The Davanzati family had gained its considerable wealth from trade. Bernardo, who had certainly not neglected the family interests, had traveled throughout Europe, and had run the family bank in Lyons. He was also a man of learning, however, and particularly loved the classics—he did a celebrated translation of Tacitus, and wrote a number of widely respected treatises. When Bernardo purchased the palazzo he was almost in his fifties; when he died in 1606, he left it to his children. It remained in the family for more than two centuries.

Beginning in 1772, the Accademia degli Armonici met in the palazzo. This academy had been founded for the encouragement of musical taste. The academicians organized concerts (Luigi Cherubini was a member); they also enjoyed the favour of the grand dukes.

The last Davanzati to own this palazzo was Carlo. Sadly, he ended his own life in 1838 by leaping from the loggia on the top floor. The Davanzati family thus died out, and the building was passed from one owner to another until, in 1904, it was purchased by Elia Volpi, a wealthy antiques dealer who had studied under Stefano Bardini. Volpi's dream was to restore an aristocratic residence of the fourteenth century, down to the tiniest details. Palazzo Davanzati suited his purposes perfectly, and Volpi

set to work restoring the building immediately. Volpi's methods may not have been philologically sound; he often resorted to reconstruction or even pure invention. Nevertheless, the result is an outstanding piece of work. The facade was restored to its original appearance, with the three great basket arches on the ground floor (in the fifteenth century, these opened onto three wool workshops), the five symmetrical windows of the second, third, and fourth floors, the many projecting pieces of wrought iron (for tying horses, to support torches and banners, to hold the staffs on which cloths were suspended or ornamental fabrics fluttered on feast days), and the great upper loggia with its jutting eaves.

Inside, walls and partitions that had been built over the course of the centuries were torn down; the more recent whitewashings were wiped away. Once again, the original features were restored to their pristine splendour: the staircase on flying buttresses; the great halls on the second and third floors, with their exquisite Gothic fireplaces and frescoed walls (often painted so as to seem upholstered in fabrics and drapes)—and above the fourth floor, the majestic covered loggia.

The painstaking restorations were completed in 1910, and Volpi decided to crown the work with a refined set of furnishings in the original style, and in some cases dating from the period concerned.

The newly restored Palazzo Davanzati quickly became the object of much public admiration; it attracted illustrious visitors, including the King of Italy. Such a great undertaking may have been the source of enormous personal satisfaction, but it was the undoing of Volpi's financial standing: quite soon (beginning in 1911) he was forced to sell much of the exquisite furniture at auction. In the end, in 1924, he sadly decided to sell the palazzo to the antiques dealer Benguiat of New York.

Benguiat, with his brother Leopoldo, did nothing more than install Gothic windows and Eastern-style columns in the cellars; they left Volpi's masterwork virtually intact (save for the furnishings sold at auction).

In 1951, the palazzo was once again put on the market; the Italian state purchased it, and in 1956 opened it to the public as the Museo della Casa Fiorentina Antica (Museum of the Early Florentine Home). This museum is unique, and it preserves the exquisite and priceless work of Elia Volpi.

Palazzo Strozzi
Piazza Strozzi 1

Directly in the heart of Florence, near the modern Piazza della Repubblica which once held the teeming Mercato Vecchio (Old Marketplace), and along the elegant Via Tornabuoni, stands a palazzo that was created through the powerful determination of one wealthy and greatly respected merchant, Filippo Strozzi. In the second half of the fifteenth century, Strozzi systematically began to purchase the houses, towers, courtyards, and lands surrounding the rectangular plot of land upon which he had decided to build his own palazzo.

Once he had completed this preliminary step, he turned his attention to a respected architect, Benedetto da Maiano. He entrusted Maiano with the task of building a palazzo that would outshine the prestigious residences built over the recent decades by the Medici, Pitti, and Rucellai families.

In 1488, Benedetto da Maiano drew up plans for a building covering a rectangular surface, divided into two symmetrical parts for separate use by Filippo Strozzi's two sons. Work actually began on July 4, 1489, and at roughly the same time, the architect Maiano, who was to have supervised construction, left for Naples.

Strozzi decided to turn to Giuliano da Sangallo; this architect quickly fashioned a wooden model of his proposal for the new Palazzo Strozzi. In time,

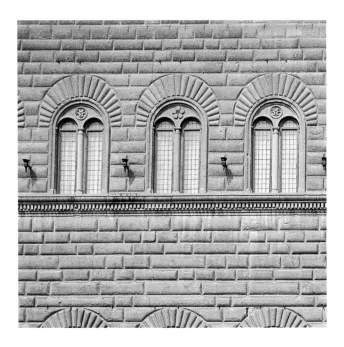

that little wooden model became famous, but there and then it failed to sway the demanding merchant, who promptly turned to yet a third architect, Simone del Pollaiolo, known as the Cronaca. And it was the Cronaca who finally succeeded in grasping and seconding the aims and ambitions of Filippo Strozzi. He developed a building with unusually tall, sheer stories; a courtyard that seemed to soar upward; a light and skillfully balanced facade (despite the symmetrical and dense texture of the rustication); and exceedingly elegant twinlight mullioned windows, each of which was crowned by an unusually tall crest of ashlars—just as the palazzo itself was crowned by an elaborate cornice that jutted far out over the street.

Under the supervision of the Cronaca, work started up again with great energy, beginning with the wing overlooking Via Tornabuoni. Within a couple of years, the ground floor was practically complete. Suddenly, on May 14, 1491, Filippo Strozzi died. The palazzo, or what existed of it, was thus passed down to the sons of the merchant. By then, however, there were three of them: Alfonso, born from Filippo's first marriage, who inherited the wing on Via Tornabuoni; and two small boys, Lorenzo and Giovanbattista (the latter was just two years old, and was known to one and all as Filippo when he grew up), born from their father's second marriage. These two latecomers were to inherit the part of the building that faced Via Strozzi and the little adjoining square (Piazzetta Strozzi). But Filippo Strozzi's will was quite strict on one point: his sons could inherit only if they continued the construction of Palazzo Strozzi.

The palazzo continued to grow: in 1495 the second floor was completed, three years later the third floor was finished, and by 1503, the courtyard too could be admired in all its elegance.

As early as 1502 the massive cornice had been completed, but only over the section of the building owned by the two younger brothers. Alfonso, caught up in intricate political machinations, was short on funds; in fact, his part of Palazzo Strozzi never was capped with its intended cornice.

When Alfonso died in 1534, without heirs, his estate passed to his two half-brothers; it seemed that Palazzo Strozzi finally belonged to a unified estate. Not for long, however. Just two years later, in 1536, the young Filippo (Giovanbattista), who openly opposed Medici rule, was sent into exile, and his property was confiscated by the state. Things went better for

Lorenzo, who had been less outspoken; still, Lorenzo was forced to halt the decoration underway under the supervision of Baccio d'Agnolo. It was not until 1568 that the grand duke Cosimo I restored—to Filippo's son Lorenzo, by then a cardinal, and to Leone, the son of the exiled Lorenzo—the part of the palazzo that had been confiscated. Thus, the building once again become the rightful property of the Strozzi family, and it regained its place in Florentine public life, with memorable parties and receptions held in its halls. There was no further construction, however, of any note. In 1652, during a meeting of a learned society called the Accademia della Crusca, the entire grand-ducal family stayed as guests of the Strozzi—Ferdinand II, with his brothers Giovan Carlo, Mattias, and Leopoldo. Despite this signal honour, the palazzo soon afterward fell into a period of relative obscurity, following the transfer of the Strozzi family to Rome.

It was not until the midnineteenth century, when Prince Ferdinando Strozzi made his definitive return to Florence with his wife Antonietta Centurione Scotto of Genoa, that Palazzo Strozzi once again became the centre of an intense social whirl.

Its renewed social standing was entirely due to the Princess Antonietta, who was the leading hostess of Florentine high society. The elder of her sons, the prince Piero, commissioned the architect Pietro Berti to build an elegant apartment in the rooms of the second floor. This apartment was entirely conceived and furnished like a sixteenth-century home, and had a fine ballroom, an armory, and a library. It was frescoed by Augusto Burchi. In the same period, Piero's wife, the wealthy Polish princess Sophia Branika, had several rooms decorated in Liberty, the Italian equivalent of art-nouveau. There she held elegant receptions.

Little survives of all that splendour. Piero died childless in 1907 and left the building to the state. There were no children, but there were rightful heirs, and they withdrew Piero's donation, selling much of the furniture and artwork to pay the inheritance taxes. The palazzo remained in the family until 1937, when it was sold to the Istituto Nazionale delle Assicurazioni, an insurance company, which completely restored it.

Palazzo Strozzi now houses such prestigious scholarly institutes as the Gabinetto Scientifico Letterario G.P. Vieusseux and the Istituto di Studi sul Rinascimento.

Palazzo Antinori
Piazzetta Antinori 3

In Florence, one palazzo in particular can rightly be held up as the paragon of the fifteenth-century palazzo built as the residence of a wealthy merchant. This is Palazzo Antinori, with its austere elegance, unostentatious appearance, well composed dimensions and geometric patterns, and painstaking detailing, which stands at one end of Via Tornabuoni, facing the church of San Michele e Gaetano Bertelde.

As early as 1461, Giovanni di Bono Boni, a leading member of the Arte del Cambio (Guild of the Moneychangers), had purchased a number of houses from a certain Messer Lionardo Bordoni; Giovanni had those houses demolished, in order to build his own house. Construction dragged

on for many years; it was still underway in 1466, when Giovanni died, still in his prime. It was Giovanni's father who oversaw the last stages of building, and the palazzo was completed in 1469. Giovanni's father also arranged to sell the newly built palazzo on July 11, 1475 to none other than Lorenzo the Magnificent. No documents survive to tell us the name of the architect who built the palazzo, but a number of clues indicate that it was probably Giuliano da Maiano.

Just a month after purchasing the palazzo, Lorenzo de' Medici sold the new property to two close friends, Carlo and Ugolino Martelli; in 1506 they in turn sold it to Niccolò di Tommaso Antinori, a merchant and a member of one of the greatest noble families of Florence. For centuries the Antinori family had lived in the quarter of Santo Spirito. Niccolò Antinori became the first member of the family to live outside of that quarter; with him came his three sons, Alessandro, Camillo, and Giovanbattista Antinori. Only Alessandro and Camillo, however, were made heirs to their father's trading company and palazzo upon his death; the third son, Giovanbattista, had given clear signs of an erratic, violent character.

Alessandro became a senator and married into the Tornabuoni family. He took it upon himself to purchase and tear down several houses adjacent to his palazzo; he then had the building enlarged, until it attained its present size, bounded by Piazza Antinori, Via delle Belle Donne, and Via del Trebbio. It was almost certainly during this renovation that the garden was laid out and that the rear elevation overlooking it was renovated. This elevation was to undergo further renovation in later years (in particular, note the four *inginocchiate* windows on the ground floor). During this first renovation, however, the facade was certainly modeled by the expert hand of Baccio d'Agnolo. One clear indication of Baccio's presence is the door leading into the garden. It is remarkably similar to another door in a similar location in Palazzo Bartolini Salimbeni, which was certainly built by Baccio. It is known, moreover, that Baccio was in close contact with the Antinori family during this period.

The branch of the Antinori family that descended from Alessandro has maintained ownership of the fifteenth-century residence, right up to the present day. Among the notables in this branch of the family, there have been several senators Niccolò di Vincenzio Antinori was one; his son, Vin-

cenzio Antinori, who married a woman from the Capponi family (Teresa Capponi), was another. Teresa Capponi was a well-read and charming woman, who made the palazzo into a welcoming haven for literati and illustrious foreigners; she also made it the site of renowned parties and receptions (the most memorable social event held in the palazzo remains the great ball of 1752; among the guests were the princes Esterházy of Galantha, and the regents of Tuscany, the princes of Craon). Then there was Niccolò Gaetano Antinori; his son Vincenzo was orphaned at age three. Vincenzo was raised by excellent guardians, who made him a learned man and a lover of the arts, devoted to scientific and mathematical studies. In time he became the director of the Gabinetto Fisico-Naturale (Cabinet of Nature and Physics, later to become a proper museum, now known as the Museo della Specola). He was also made a member of the editorial staff, for his scientific expertise, of the *Vocabolario della Crusca*, Italy's great national dictionary. And he was selected by the grand duke Leopoldo II as a tutor for the ducal children.

Following the unification of Italy and the exile of the Lorraine dynasty, Vincenzo Antinori, who had never allowed himself to be dragged into politics, took refuge in retirement, surrounded by the numerous family that still looks down upon us from a painting by Giuseppe Bezzuoli, hanging in a corridor on the third floor of the palazzo.

His descendants have undertaken structural restorations of their prestigious home on more than one occasion. The most recent restoration was quite substantial; it was carried out under the supervision of architect Emilio Dori. Following the move of the British Institute and the British Consulate—which had long occupied the second floor of the palazzo—to new quarters, Dori and his workers restored the general silhouette, the roofs and ceilings, and various original structures. The restoration was an admirable success.

The third floor is elegantly furnished, and is used as a swank reception area; the ground floor has been converted into a renowned *cantinetta*, or wine cellar, where visitors can sample the excellent wines produced by the Antinori vineyards.

Palazzo Venturi Ginori
Via della Scala 85

To speak of this palazzo in terms that are chronologically correct, we must begin with the garden, or better, from the ancient *orto*, the Latin *hortus*. In 1482 a sister of Lorenzo the Magnificent, Nannina, was married to Bernardo di Messer Giovanni Rucellai, thus acquiring all the lands in the surrounding area. The area in question was marshland watered by the nearby river Mugnone. For centuries, landholdings here belonged to the Donati, Acciaiuoli, and Gianfigliazzi families, as well as numerous other illustrious clans. In 1186, a *leprosarium*, or leper's hospital, was built here; at the end of the fifteenth century, it was the only building that

stood in this entire area. For the first twenty years of his ownership, Bernardo Rucellai simply farmed the land, as had been done before him, raising vegetables and fruit in the Orti Oricellari, as they were called (from a Latinized version of the name Rucellai). Then, toward the end of the fifteenth century, Bernardo decided to have a *casino* built there, a pastoral party house for the Rucellai family, designed by Leon Battista Alberti. Bernardo later had the building and gardens adorned with busts, statues, and ancient sarcophagi. At the corner of Via della Scala and Via degli Orti Oricellari stood a handsome Della Robbia Madonna.

Bernardo had special ties with the Medici family, and for many years he welcomed to his Casino all members of the Accademia delle Arti e delle Scienze (Academy of Arts and Sciences) who enjoyed the patronage and

encouragement of the Medici. When Bernardo Rucellai died in 1514, the Palazzo degli Orti Oricellari was inherited by his two sons, Giovanni (who died in 1525) and Palla. When Palla was forced into exile in 1527, in conjunction with the expulsion of the Medici from Florence, the palazzo and its grounds were ransacked and devastated. When the family returned to Florence, they remained owners of the Casino until 1573, when it was sold to Bianca Cappello, the mistress of the grand duke Francesco I. Upon her death, the new grand duke Ferdinand I made a gift of the Casino to Don Antonio de' Medici, who in turn rented it to the ambassador of the Venetian Republic.

In 1608 the Casino became the property of Giannantonio Orsini, and it remained in the Orsini family until 1640, when it returned to the Medici family, becoming the home of the cardinal Giovan Carlo de' Medici. This cardinal was the brother of the grand duke Ferdinand II; he had the palazzo decorated with series of frescoes by Pietro Berrettini da Cortona and Angelo Michele Colonna. The cardinal then moved his precious gallery of paintings there, with works by Raphael, Tintoretto, Titian, and Filippo Lippi. Finally he commissioned Antonio Novelli to build the fountains in the garden, the Cavern of Polyphemus, and a colossal statue of Polyphemus (Cyclops), made of brick and stucco, but so highly polished as to seem like marble.

When the cardinal died in 1663, the grand duke was forced to sell the Casino in order to liquidate his debts, and it was purchased by the marchese Ferdinando Ridolfi, who hired Pier Francesco Silvani to enlarge the residence. The Casino remained in the Ridolfi family until 1765, when it came by inheritance into the hands of Giuseppe Stiozzi. Stiozzi decided to build a Romantic, Englishstyle garden with the assistance of the count and architect Luigi de Cambray-Digny. The Casino changed ownership again, passing from the Stiozzi family to Princess Olga Orloff in 1861. Under her ownership, the architect Giuseppe Poggi restored the building to its original appearance, while the main hall was decorated by Leopoldo Costoli with medallions depicting all the leading thinkers of the time. At the end of the nineteenth century, the building and the garden became possessions of the marchese Ippolito Venturi Ginori, then were inherited by his son Roberto, who died in 1965.

NON TVRBINO ALLA QVIETE I SVOI RIPOSI

LARVE IMPORTVNE
E SOGNI SPAVENTOSI

Palazzo Rucellai
Via della Vigna Nuova 18

With the construction of the Palazzo Medici (now Palazzo Medici Riccardi) on Via Larga (now Via Cavour), civil architecture in the city of Florence took a radical new direction. In this context, one of the first and most significant developments was certainly the palazzo built on Via della Vigna Nuova at the behest of Giovanni Rucellai, a respected merchant and renowned patron of the arts. Although he was the son-in-law of Palla Strozzi, who had shown himself to be a bitter rival of the Medici, Rucellai succeeded in maintaining friendly relations with the burgeoning new dynasty; he even succeeded in building a fortune for his own family. Around 1450 he asked the architect Leon Battista Alberti to build him a

fitting home. The result is a palazzo with an unusual facade in which elements from Roman antiquity (the socle with a rhomboid pattern, the small square windows, the symmetrically stacked architectural orders) blend perfectly with decidedly more modern features (the high twin-light mullioned windows on the two top floors, the flat rustication). The supervising architect was in all likelihood Bernardo Rossellino. At first, plans had called for a facade with five vertical bays with a central door, but the number of vertical bays of windows was increased to seven; and a new portal was built, establishing a new if imperfect symmetry.

Giovanni Rucellai had two sons, Pandolfo, the elder, and Bernardo, who was born in 1448. It was on the occasion of the very prestigious wedding of Bernardo and one of the sisters of Lorenzo the Magnificent, Lucrezia de' Medici, known as Nannina, in June of 1446, that the palazzo had its house-warming, as it were. Decked out for the gala, the palazzo overlooked a stage occupying the entire *piazzetta*, adorned with flowers and compositions in fruit. There was dancing and banqueting for three days. Across from his new palazzo, Rucellai also erected an elegant loggia with three arches, punctuated by tall pillars, which was probably also designed by Leon Battista Alberti. This loggia, in keeping with the customs of the time, was used for the haggling and accounting of business and trade, as well as for private meetings and family celebrations. Over the centuries, this loggia was enclosed—transformed into a closed room that served in the seventeenth century as the studio of the renowned sculptor Giovanni Battista Foggini—and opened again more than once; it is now enclosed by large plate-glass windows that do not hide the structure, and is an ideal exhibition space.

The descendants of Giovanni Rucellai still live in the palazzo. That family has included humanists, senators, historians, and a member of the Accademia Colombaria, who allowed the prestigious institution to hold its meetings in the palazzo.

In the middle of the eighteenth century, Giuseppe Rucellai used his wedding to Teresa de' Pazzi as an opportunity to greatly embellish the entire *piano nobile*, or main upper floor. Worthy of note in these rooms are the frescoes, primarily by Gian Domenico Ferretti.

More renovations and restorations were completed throughout the nine-

teenth century and in the early twentieth century; of particular signifi-
cance was the lengthening of the main staircase, which had originally
reached up only as high as the *piano nobile*. The third floor, in fact, had
originally been intended as a storage area and servants' quarters. It was
only later that residential apartments were installed on that floor.

At the turn of the twentieth century, the second floor was the residence
of Count Giulio Rucellai and the Countess Lysin, widow of the Prince
Woronzow; they were well known for their frequent and spectacular parties. On the third floor lived Count Cosimo Rucellai and his wife, Edith
Bronson, an American by birth. She and Cosimo were the forebears of
the current owners of the palazzo. Still higher up, above the cornice and
practically invisible from the street, is a loggia with a balustrade where
there was once an open garden. Later, enclosed and given a dropped
ceiling, it became an inhabitable suite, and it still crowns this unusual
palazzo.

Palazzo Della Gherardesca

Borgo Pinti 99

In the fifteenth century a man born into the family of a lowly miller in Colle Val d'Elsa traveled to Florence, and there succeeded in rising through the ranks, attaining a remarkable series of honours until he became the secretary of the Florentine Republic in 1468, and Gonfalonier of Justice in 1486. This man, Bartolommeo Scala, became the target of much criticism from eminent citizens. Although it was probably his rapid rise and his determined personality that drew the attacks, he was specifically accused of having used public funds to build himself a palazzo near the city walls.

The chain of events that led to his accusation began in 1472, when Lorenzo de' Medici ordered Scala to draw up a legal bill of confiscation for the lands and possessions of religious orders around the city walls. These religious landholdings were hindering the much-needed expansion of Florence. As a result of the confiscations, much of this land was deeded to private citizens. Among the land was a plot near the gate of Porta a Pinti, at the end of the Borgo Pinti; Bartolommeo Scala purchased this plot of land from the Spedale degli Innocenti, or foundling hospital. In 1480 a palazzo already stood on this land, and Bartolommeo Scala lived in it with his family.

The architect who had been hired to build it was certainly Giuliano da Sangallo. Based on the few existing buildings, Giuliano da Sangallo had created a home suspended between city and countryside, open to the surrounding greenery, a long and exceedingly well-lit palazzo. One particularly noteworthy feature is the courtyard, elegantly embroidered with stucco basreliefs. It is also bedecked with porticoes with broad arches, and side walls that are low enough to allow a generous amount of daylight to reach the interior.

The Scala family handed down the palazzo and its grounds from father to son for about a century. Finally, Giulio Scala, whose offspring included three daughters (all withdrew to nunneries) and no sons, arranged for the girls to sell the building and adjacent grounds to Alessandro Cardinal de' Medici upon his own death. And that is precisely what happened in 1585.

The new owner wasted no time in renovating and embellishing the palazzo. Frescoes were painted in the halls, ornaments and decorations were installed in the courtyard, and special attention was devoted to the chapel on the ground floor (here, the architect Giovanni Stradano, or Jan Van der Straet, worked in 1586 and 1587). When the new owner became pope in 1605, with the name of Leo XI, he left Florence permanently for Rome. The former cardinal made a gift of the palazzo to his sister, Costanza, the wife of Ugo Della Gherardesca. The Della Gherardesca family was an old family of counts of Donoratico, and had deep roots and feudal possessions along the Tyrrhenian coast, between Pisa and the Maremma; the family did not settle in Florence until the mid-sixteenth century.

The Della Gherardesca family gave its name to the palazzo in Borgo Pin-

ti, and was responsible for the palazzo's present-day appearance. In fact, around 1720, another count Ugo Della Gherardesca ordered major renovations. The entire palazzo was radically altered, and only the courtyard preserved its fifteenth-century appearance. The facades overlooking the street and the garden were rebuilt, and given a uniform style by the architect Antonio Ferri. Ferri added a number of windows on the ground floor (originally there had only been two), and rebuilt the original loggia. He added two massive forward wings on either side of the loggia. The large portal—surmounted by a balcony and coat-of-arms—was also added in the eighteenth century, as were the frescoes and stuccoes in the halls and gallery on the second floor (done by Alessandro Geri).

The modifications of the garden date from the nineteenth century. Until then, only the area directly behind the palazzo could be described as a garden; the rest of the grounds were planted with vegetable gardens and fruit orchards. It was the count Guido Alberto Della Gherardesca who decided, around 1820, to create a single Romantic-style garden, in accordance with the tastes of the time. This garden was dotted with small Ionic and Doric temples, was crisscrossed by artistically modeled paths and meadows, and was punctuated with statues and copses. The entire project was overseen by Giuseppe Cacialli, Antonio Martini, and Ottavio Giovannozzi.

Fifty years later, another Della Gherardesca, the count Ugolino, was faced with the demolition of Florence's city walls, and the construction of the new Viale Principe Amedeo, a broad avenue that ran right along the northern side of the garden. He therefore hired the architect Giuseppe Poggi to design and build the monumental gate and the buildings that still enclose the garden on the northern side.

The heirs of count Ugolino sold the estate to Ismail Pasha, the former viceroy of Egypt. In turn, Ismail Pasha sold the estate to the Società delle Strade Ferrate Meridionali, a public works agency. In 1940 the estate was acquired by its present owner, the Società Metallurgica Italiana, an industrial corporation. SMI has done considerable restoration of the courtyard and the rooms on the ground floor and second floor; these rooms, with the lush adjoining gardens, constitute one of the most spectacular and interesting architectural complexes in Florence.

Palazzo Gondi
Piazza San Firenze 2

Few visitors know that the sloping ground at the foot of the Palazzo Vecchio, along Via della Ninna and Via dei Gondi, is an indication of the tiers
of seats of the ancient Roman theatre buried beneath; all subsequent construction has been forced to take this underlying slope into account.
Among the buildings in question is the palazzo overlooking Piazza San
Firenze, built at the end of the fifteenth century by Giuliano da Sangallo, on behalf of Giuliano di Lionardo Gondi. This latter individal was a
merchant who had made a fortune trading in Naples; there he had also
won the esteem and benevolence of the king, Ferdinand of Aragon. And
so, when Gondi decided to return to his native Florence, the new king
Alfonso, son of Ferdinand, made Gondi a duke.

In Naples, Gondi had made the acquaintance of Giuliano da Sangallo,
who was working there on behalf of the court of Aragon. Gondi summoned da Sangallo in 1489 when he decided to build a palazzo that
would be a fitting residence for his own family. The Gondi family owned
many houses in the quarter of Santa Maria Novella; many of their storehouses, however, were located in the quarter of Santa Croce. Here, the
new duke Giuliano purchased a number of new houses from the city government, from the Arti, and from the Giugni family; he demolished these
buildings and leveled an area on which to build his new home.

The palazzo he built was smaller than the one we now see. With six vertical bays of windows on two stories, it possessed two doors, one of them
set in the first vertical bay on the right, the other in the fourth vertical
bay. We know from the will of Duke Giuliano Gondi, who died in 1501,
that he had already taken up residence in the palazzo with his family, but
that construction was not finished. The heirs, in fact, still had to oversee
and pay for the completion of the palazzo. We do not know what the final
stages in construction involved. Some think that the palazzo had yet to be
extended toward Palazzo Vecchio, so as to incorporate the other buildings
that the Gondi family already owned in the area. Others theorize that the
palazzo had to be extended, but in the opposite direction, toward Via
Condotta, by the addition of three vertical bays of windows, to give the

distinctly asymmetrical doors a central location. In any case, the extension of the palazzo was never completed. The most notable feature of the facade was the intricate motif and texture of the rustication. Also greatly admired was the balconied terrace that surmounted the palazzo, replacing the cornice. Most of all, however, attention focused on the stupendous courtyard, one of da Sangallo's greatest creations. The courtyard is perfectly geometrical and linear; its crowning touch is the handsome staircase, embellished with exquisitely cut stone bas-reliefs.

Between the sixteenth and seventeenth centuries the prestige of the Gondi family grew, both in Florence and elsewhere. Many family members were made senators; others moved to France and were made dukes of Retz; these emigrants helped their Florentine relatives establish solid contacts in Paris. Some Florentine Gondis were sent to Paris as ambassadors.

If the family reputation flourished and grew, the palazzo remained static and unchanged. The sole exception was the lovely fountain installed in the courtyard in 1652 by another Giuliano Gondi, as a *perfezionamento*, a crowning touch. A significant new development came about in 1686, however, when the property was inherited by the two sons of Amerigo Gondi, Vincenzio and Angelo. These two sons summoned the architect Antonio Ferri and asked him to renovate the entire portion of the palazzo located behind the courtyard. This led to the construction of the stables and a series of rooms—nicely decorated and frescoed by fashionable artists, from Matteo Bonechi to Lorenzo del Moro—that included a splendid bedroom, where Angelo brought his new bride, Elisabetta Cerretani. Two centuries passed before further major structural changes were made in the palazzo. In 1870, in the midst of the general renovation of the historic centre of Florence, the decision was made to widen the exceedingly narrow Via dei Gondi, alongside the Palazzo Vecchio; the few small buildings that the family owned in this area were confiscated and demolished. The marchese Eugenio Gondi took this opportunity to have the architect Giuseppe Poggi fulfill the last wishes of his ancestor Giuliano Gondi by completing the palazzo. Poggi brilliantly resolved the challenge by adding a vertical bay of windows on the south side of the facade. In so doing he added a door, and thus restored a sense of symmetry to the entire building. He also completed a facade with five vertical bays of windows and three doors overlooking the Via dei Gondi. He used stone from the quarries of Monteripaldi and Altomena that fit particularly well with the stone that had been used by Giuliano da Sangallo. He built a stone staircase that led from the *porte cochère* directly up to the *piano nobile*. These changes gave the palazzo its present-day appearance.

After Poggi, only the architect Emilio Dori in the twentieth century did any further renovation; he adapted the rooms on the second and third floors for use as offices and studios. The residence of the owners was installed on the fourth floor, which was originally intended as a storage area and attic; it had a splendid little loggia, to which were added a number of terraces, which still make the cozy apartment one of the most panoramic homes in all of Florence.

Palazzo Ximenes da Sangallo
Borgo Pinti 68

Giuliano and Antonio Giamberti were two respected architects in late-fif-teenth-century Florence; they are remembered by their working names as Giuliano and Antonio da Sangallo. Around 1490, they began to purchase plots of land along the street of Borgo Pinti. According to the census of the Florentine Republic, Giuliano had already built a house on that land as early as 1498. Rather than speaking of a house—or *casa*—in the narrow sense of the term, however, we should probably refer to a palazzo, given that by the year 1510 Vasari says the building was widely renowned for the paintings that hung in its halls and rooms (among them were paintings by Botticelli and Paolo Uccello), and for the Roman antiquities that were on display throughout.

In 1603 the descendants of Giuliano's son, Francesco da Sangallo, sold

the *casa* to Sebastian di Tommaso Ximenes de Aragona, scion of a family of Castilian and Portuguese origin; he had made his fortune in Lisbon through a thriving trading concern he had set up there. Tommaso came to Florence in the early seventeenth century, with his brothers Ferdinando and Emanuele, and soon managed to secure the title of Lord of the town of Saturnia. He was also made senator and, most important, won his way into the favour of the grand duke. It came as little surprise then that his son Sebastiano won the hand of Caterina, the daughter of Raffaello de' Medici, from the branch of the Marchesi di Castellina. Sebastiano, in order to further cement his well consolidated social standing, decided to purchase the palazzo of the da Sangallo family. Again, it was not surprising that, once Sebastiano had purchased the palazzo, he consulted an acclaimed architect, Gherardo Silvani, and asked him to enlarge the building and renovate the facade. Small traces of Silvani's work can

still be seen in the central vertical bay of the main facade, and in the five windows that are symmetrically arranged there, on several stories.

With the passage of the decades and the succession of a series of members of the Ximenes de Aragona family as owners of the palazzo, the halls on the *piano nobile* were embellished and decorated, culminating in the elegant ornaments of the renowned ball room.

Among the illustrious guests who stayed in this refined home, let us mention one in particular, the young general Napoleon Bonaparte. In June of 1796 Bonaparte had been invited to Florence by the resident minister of the French Republic who worked and lived out of a suite of rooms on the *piano nobile* of Palazzo Ximenes. Here the future emperor spent the night in a comfortable bed chamber, waiting to be received by the grand duke.

In the nineteenth century, the line of male descendants of the Ximenes de Aragona family died out, and the family home, handed down through the female descendants, passed through many different hands. In 1816, the last male Ximenes, Ferdinando, left it in his will to the sons of his sister, Bandino and Pietro Leopoldo Panciatichi.

This family only owned the palazzo for a few decades, but that was long enough for Maria Anna Paolucci Panciatichi to create a notable garden, with well tended groves of trees, and have one of the facades overlooking the adjacent park redone in full seventeenth-century style. Maria Anna Paolucci Panciatichi was also responsible for having much of the palazzo enlarged and rebuilt, while the size of the grounds was reduced by the new road running nearby, the Via Giusti.

At the end of the nineteenth century, the property was inherited by the counts of San Giorgio, and a few years later, by the counts of Arrigoni degli Oddi. Thus, when the countess Oddina married Prince Francesco Ruffo di Scilla, the palazzo formed part of her dowry.

Their descendants and heirs still live in the venerable mansion, in the lovely and well furnished rooms of the *piano nobile*, with a rich and renowned gallery of paintings.

Palazzo Cocchi
Piazza Santa Croce 1

Directly across from the basilica of Santa Croce—on the site of an ancient Roman theatre which is reflected in the layout of many streets in the area—once stood most of the houses that belonged to the Peruzzi family in the thirteenth and fourteenth centuries. Some of those houses were purchased later in the fifteenth century by the Cocchi Donati family, who wished to build their own palazzo on the site. Some scholars believe that they hired the architect Baccio d'Agnolo to design and build their palazzo. Others believe the attribution is inaccurate because civic records may date the construction to the years between 1470 and 1480, and Baccio was born in 1462. There is no doubt, however, that the

facade of Palazzo Cocchi has always generated heated debate and curiosity among artists and scholars, because of its singular form and appearance. The facade clearly incorporates features of an existing four-teenth-century building that was subsumed in the new palazzo (in par-ticular, on the ground floor, note the projections and ashlars). The most interesting aspects of the building, however, are to be found on the upper floors, which juxtapose a series of geometric patterns with architectural features such as the flattened pilaster strips, cornicework, arches, win-dows with or without architraves, and twin-light mullioned windows. Each of these elements stands independently, and yet together they form a whole that is oddly harmonious.

The extremely geometrical composition has led some to propose Giuliano da Sangallo as the architect, when he was newly returned from Rome, where he had been studyings classical architecture. Plausible though this may be, and though clear similarities with other work by the great archi-tect seem to support it, it remains a hypothesis.

The Cocchi Donati family had been particularly respected during the Flo-rentine Republic, and had ties with the Da Fortuna and the Sangalletti families. They maintained ownership of the palazzo until the second half of the eighteenth century, when the last descendent of the family, Mad-dalena, wife of the marchese Ottavio Orazio Pucci, died. Her daughter, Lucrezia, brought the palazzo as her dowry when she married a Serris-tori, and the Serristori family owned it throughout the nineteenth centu-ry. During these centuries, no changes were made in the building's struc-ture. Only the interior was frescoed, in conformity with the tastes of the eighteenth and nineteenth centuries. These frescoes survive, in part. In 1892 the palazzo—which had become part of the estate of the Della Seta family, in the dowry of Maddalena Serristori, who married the count Andrea Agostini Della Seta—was sold to the city of Florence, which used it as a school building. Only recently has it been adapted for use as a city office building.

Palazzo Capponi delle Rovinate
Via de' Bardi 36

The Capponi family has always been one of the most respected in Florence. In every chapter of Florentine history, the Capponi have distinguished themselves, either for the high offices they held (Priori and Gonfalonieri, high public offices, during the Florentine Republic; Senators under the Principality; and cardinals and prelates in every period), or for the great deeds they performed. And that is without even mentioning Senator Gino Capponi, who played a major role in the city's nineteenth-century history, prior to and under the new Kingdom of Italy. The Capponi family soon split up into different branches, and then established ties of marriage with virtually all of the leading families of Florence. It was widely thought in these families that the addition of a Capponi to their ranks through marriage heightened their nobility. As a result the Capponi family had a great many prestigious homes scattered through-

out Florence, from Santo Spirito to San Frediano, from Via Larga (the present-day Via Cavour) to the street that was one day to be known as Via Gino Capponi.

The first palazzo to be inhabited by the Capponi family, however, is the one on Via de' Bardi (still owned by a branch of the Capponi family), conventionally called Palazzo Capponi delle Rovinate because the hill that looms above it has been subject to disastrous landslides (*rovinate*) more than once. Because of the destruction and deaths that ensued, Cosimo I de' Medici decreed around 1550 that it was forbidden to build new houses there. Although we have no evidence that this attribution is well founded, the palazzo does have a number of interesting and noteworthy

features. First of all, let us consider the facade, which is unusual for the rustication seen on the ground floor, which seems to foreshadow much of the work done by Michelozzo and Brunelleschi. There are still marks of the three large projecting openings, typical of fourteenth-century buildings, which were clearly later closed up. That was not the only major work done on the facade just note the two *inginocchiate* windows and the numerous cornices of the other windows, which do not hamper the rigorous linear appearance of the facade, embellished symmetrically on either end by two heraldic crests of the da Uzzano family.

The palazzo has another remarkable aspect: there is a second, radically different facade in the rear, overlooking the Arno. This facade was built

by the architect Giuseppe Poggi in the midnineteenth century when, in the context of the general renovation and beautification of central Florence, the composite and symmetrical facade overlooking the Arno seemed out of place. With the approval of the two counts—Luigi and Ferdinando—the facade was altered to its present form, with two broad side balconies that provide illumination to the rooms within. Another noteworthy feature, ahead of its time, is the courtyard. The fourteenth-century-style *graffiti*, the stylized foliate capitals, the cross vaults, are balanced by the square shape and the broad porticoes, already alluding to fifteenth-century architecture. There are notable rooms on the second floor as well, starting with the enormous *salone* with four windows. This large room has interesting decorations, typically eighteenth-century in technique and subject, featuring landscapes and scenes of battle. Adjoining it are two drawing rooms, the Salotto Rosso and the Salotto Giallo.

In the Salotto Giallo there hangs a large, notable collection of paintings, a clear demonstration of the special love the Capponi family has always shown for art. In fact, in the eighteenth-century chapel that opens onto the Salotto Rosso, there hangs a Pontormo Madonna, alongside a beautiful piece of religious stained glass dating from the sixteenth century, a curious collection of relics, and a fresco that is generally thought to date from the time of the da Uzzano family. In fact, the palazzo was owned by that family for decades, until Agnolo da Uzzano, the son of Niccolò, left the palazzo in the mid-fifteenth century to his cousin Niccolò, the son of Pier Capponi and Dianora da Uzzano. From that time on the building was handed from one branch to another, but it always remained in the same family—that of the Capponi. (It remained the property of the heirs of Niccolò until the seventeenth century, then it was inherited by Ferrante Capponi, a member of a collateral branch, and from him to another line; a member of that line was the other Ferrante, who paid for restorations and frescoes throughout the *piano nobile* in the first half of the eighteenth century). And the palazzo still belongs to the Capponi family today, who preserve its remarkable architectural, pictorial, and decorative details, as well as its furnishings.

Casino Torrigiani del Campuccio
Via de' Serragli 144

In the crowded quarter of Oltrarno, amidst the dense crisscrossing welter of streets, lanes, and alleys, there lies, unbeknownst to the passerby, one of the largest parks in Florence. Protected on one side by the walls and buildings of Via de' Serragli and on the other side by one of the few surviving fragments of the ancient ring of Florence's city walls, this huge garden offers virtually no outward signs of its presence. And yet, when the Torrigiani family purchased their first houses and their first orchards and vegetable gardens on Via del Campuccio, the area was hardly considered a particularly elegant one, or even a residential area at all. Stagnant water rendered the site unhealthy, because adequate drainage and irrigation was lacking. The very air was considered bad as a result, and harmful to one's health. Still, the Torrigiani family was not easily daunted, and they tenaciously pursued their objective they planned to build an

elegant *casino*, a country lodge midway between the open countryside and the crowded city, with a pleasant view of vast stretches of greenery. Here, in accordance with the customs of the period, parties could be organized, leisurely afternoons could be spent, and refuge could be found from the baking summer heat of the city.

Raffaello Torrigiani was the first member of the family to buy property in this area; he purchased two houses and a vegetable plot. His son, Luca Torrigiani, followed Raffaello's example, acquiring other plots of land in the same zone. The family soon undertook reclamation work; work also began on the enlargement and renovation of the existing buildings. And so, by the end of the sixteenth century, a large and aristocratic residence already stood, overlooking Via del Campuccio. Before long the renown of the Orti dei Torrigiani began to spread, establishing a reputation for high-quality farm products. Greater still was the growing reputation of the family home for the parties and festivals that were held in the section of the gardens planted with little groves of cedar and jasmine trees.

In 1777 Luigi Cardinal Torrigiani died, the last male heir to the family property, leaving the entire estate to his little grand-nephew, Pietro Guadagni, the four-year-old son of Teresa Torrigiani. When the little boy had grown, he took his mother's surname, and showed a particular attention to, and interest in the garden, which he soon enlarged. Between 1802 and 1817 he purchased the land just beyond the garden walls. On this land stood, and still stand, the "second walls" built by Cosimo I de' Medici as added fortification for the city. In the same years, Pietro purchased a *casino* from the Del Rosso family, with a long avenue that ran into Via de' Serragli; upon this land was built the villa that stands in the centre of the present-day garden. Lastly, he purchased yet another *casino* that also overlooked Via de' Serragli. Thus, in that fifteen-year period, the grounds attained their present size and extension, reaching as far as Porta Romana, and covering ten full hectares.

The architect Luigi Cambray-Digny, later succeded by Gaetano Baccani, worked to transform the appearance of the estate, creating a perfect Romantic-style garden: three aristocratic homes, avenues, large plazas, flowerbeds (one of which was particularly large, circular, and was encompassed by a horsetrack; it has always been known as the *Ippodromo*), and

a large tower built by Baccani. This tower was meant as a concrete manifestation of the Torrigiani family escutcheon. In it was installed a *gabinetto di macchine astronomiche* (studio of astronomic machinery). Also dotting the estate were little classical temples and even a Grotta di Merlino (Merlin's Grotto). In a short time this became one of the most renowned places in Florence, particularly popular with foreign visitors. When a number of suites in the villas were made available for rental in the nineteenth century, foreign visitors snapped them up. Lady Charlotte Campbell, daughter of a Duke of Argyll; Prince Gustav Vasa, descended from King Vasa of Sweden; and the Count de La Rochefoucauld were all

able to admire the vast botanical gardens, tended with zealous care by small armies of gardeners.

Even today, although the garden has been split up due to the technical demands of succession and inheritance among the many branches of the family, the Giardino Torrigiani remains a place of great charm, as well as a working garden with a notable nursery. Indeed, it is quite easy to understand why the son of Marchese Pietro Torrigiani chose to erect a monument to him in the heart of the immense garden that he did so much to nurture and preserve.

Palazzo Nonfinito
Via del Proconsolo 12

The houses set at the corner of Via del Proconsolo and Borgo degli Albizzi belonged for many years to the Pazzi family; indeed this street corner was known as the Canto dei Pazzi. It was this same Pazzi family that linked its name to the inglorious and unsuccessful conspiracy against the Medici in 1478. On November 10, 1592, all of the houses were purchased by Alessandro Strozzi, son of the senator Camillo Strozzi; Alessandro had them torn down to make way for his own new palazzo.

He summoned the architect Bernardo Buontalenti, and had him design the ground floor with its distinctive *inginocchiate* windows and the entire *piano nobile*. Actual construction began on July 15, 1593, and many master craftsmen worked on the building. The cost of the project soon spiraled out of control, and Alessandro Strozzi realized that he could not finance it by himself. He therefore decided to involve his half-brother, Roberto, the son born out of wedlock of Alessandro's father Camillo. Camillo had declared Roberto to be his legitimate son, and sent him to Venice to engage in commerce, and Roberto had succeeded brilliantly in his new trade. In 1596 Roberto purchased half of the estate; the following year he purchased the other half, thus becoming sole owner.

Roberto had long resided in the Veneto, and he at first planned to entrust the completion of the project to an architect from that part of Italy: Vincenzo Scamozzi. The choice did not yield the hoped-for results, and soon Tuscan architects were again supervising construction. Giovanni Caccini completed the facades and the portal that opened onto Via del Proconsolo; he also created the large coat-of-arms that can be seen high over the corner of the two streets. Vignola worked on the part of the second floor that over looks Via del Proconsolo.

Ludovico Cardi, known as the Cigoli, built the courtyard. Santi di Tito da Sansepolcro was responsible for the monumental staircase, clearly influenced by similar structures built by Vasari.

The work of so many illustrious architects, however, led to steadily rising costs, and once again the owner was faced with what seems to have been a recurring situation in the history of this palazzo Roberto Strozzi ran out

of money and was forced to suspend construction. As a result, parts of the courtyard and the mezzanine above the second floor remained unfinished. Thus the palazzo got its name—Palazzo Nonfinito, the unfinished palazzo. Various collateral branches of the Strozzi family handed this prestigious home down over the generations, without completing construction or beautifying the interior. At last, in 1802, the palazzo was purchased by Giovanni di Francesco Guasti; twelve years later he in turn sold it to the government of Tuscany. It was thus that Palazzo Nonfinito became the headquarters of the Ministry of the Interior and the feared police force under the House of Lorraine. Following the unification of Italy, it housed the Consiglio di Stato (Council of State) during the brief period when Florence was capital of Italy. It then became property of the Italian Postal and Telegraphic Service. Since 1920 it has been the site of the Istituto di Antropologia e Etnologia of the Università di Firenze. This institute was founded in 1869 by Paolo Mantegazza.

Palazzo Bartolini Salimbeni

Piazza Santa Trinita 1

The Bartolini Salimbeni family was originally from Siena, but they moved to Florence at the turn of the fourteenth century and soon became respected Florentine citizens and were active in the city's political life. Members of the family held public office many times, and they were supporters of the Medici, as well as intimates of that family. They had amassed enormous wealth in the silk trade.

When Giovanni di Bartolomeo di Leonardo Bartolini Salimbeni decided to build a palazzo for himself directly across from the church of Santa Trinita, just a stone's throw from Palazzo Feroni, he also decided—good businessman that he was—to keep a ledger of all the expenses and payments, the *Libro della Muraglia*. The first entry bears the date of February 27, 1519 (this was actually 1520, because the Florentine year began on March 25).

This ledger is a treasure trove of information. It informs us, for instance, that Giovanni Bartolini, as he signed his name, purchased houses and workshops in the area in which he planned to build for the sum of 1,929 florins, and that he then had those buildings torn down. We further know that from the very beginning of construction, the project was entrusted to the respected architect Baccio d'Agnolo, who worked on the project until May 28, 1523, when construction was largely complete. By this time, total costs amounted to roughly 10,000 florins.

These three years of hard work produced an exceedingly original palazzo; so original, in fact, that a hail of criticism and even harsh attacks poured down upon the architect. The facade in particular prompted much discussion: it was too innovative for its time, with its jutting eaves and stringcourse cornices marking each floor, with its slender columns flanking the portal, with its triangular pediments atop door and windows. Baccio d'Agnolo responded cleverly to the attacks. On the pediment that topped the portal, he carved a Latin inscription that reads *Carpere promptius quam imitari* (It is easier to criticize than to imitate). In the end, time proved the architect right his forward-looking approach found numerous fervent imitators in successive decades.

114

On the facade of the palazzo, specifically on the cross-bars of the windows, another inscription reads *Per non dormire* (Lest we sleep), the motto of the Bartolini Salimbeni family. This motto refers to a story concerning a member of the family, who, in order to be the first one to market and purchase a shipment of silk at an excellent price, drugged the wine of his closest rivals with opium. Note the unmistakable blooms of opium poppies along the friezes that run the length of the building.

If the facade overlooking Santa Trinita was the most controversial, the facade on Via Porta Rossa is also worthy of mention. Note the majestic portal, the crossed windows, and the oculi just beneath the eaves. All three different types of stone used in sixteenth-century Florence were employed in the facade: *pietra serena, pietraforte,* and *pietra bigia.* This is a noteworthy and unusual feature.

In spite of the initial harsh criticism of the facade, there was only praise for the elegant courtyard. Originally porticoed on three sides, the courtyard featured a small and finely decorated loggia on the second floor. There was also a loggia on the top floor, surmounted, oddly enough, by a second loggia facing south. *Graffiti* decorations adorned the walls up to the third floor. Also worthy of note is the staircase, with its original stone handrail. The rooms in the top floors are squeezed into the limited space available, within the area bounded by the two streets below.

The Bartolini Salimbeni family lived continuously in this palazzo until 1839, and then rented it out, as was fairly common practice in that period. The palazzo thus became one of the prestigious hotels in Florence, the Hôtel du Nord; among the celebrities who stopped here was the American writer Herman Melville. In 1863, the palazzo was sold to Prince Pius of Savoy, and in ensuing decades sections of the palazzo were sold to the Malvezzi, Sanvitale, Laparelli, and Franzoni families, until the entire estate was purchased by the Marchesi Salina Amorini of Bologna. At one point the palazzo was used as the French consulate. In 1961 it was thoroughly and painstakingly restored, which partly halted the deterioration of the magnificent sixteenth century facade.

Palazzo Bargellini, formerly Palazzo da Verrazzano
Via delle Pinzochere 3

In the heart of the ancient quarter of Santa Croce, wedged into the dense welter of houses crowded one against another, on the secluded Via delle Pinzochere (the name of the street comes from a convent of Franciscan tertiary nuns that once stood in this quarter), stands a large, austere palazzo, marked by its broad streetside bench. This is the venerable old residence of the da Verrazzano family. It still has a number of original and interesting features the bench; the large windows on the two top floors, surrounded by round arches made of flat ashlars; the unusually pronounced, jutting eaves that extend nearly halfway over the street below. The courtyard, too, is quite spectacular. It was originally porticoed symmetrically on two sides, but only the portico nearest the entrance survives, decorated with exquisite capitals topping the columns. From the courtyard, one enters a small but enchanting garden, which, although it has been enlarged over the centuries, can be described as a tiny niche set in a surrounding wreath of buildings, tucked away and hidden amidst the taller structures. One would never guess from outside that the garden is there, despite the magnificent trees that have grown in it for centuries. The staircase that runs up to the *piano nobile*, with its original stone handrail, is also quite remarkable; even more so is the spiral staircase, also made of stone, that runs from the cellar up to the topmost floor of the palazzo.

It is not known with any certainty who designed and built this palazzo. Many scholars have suggested Baccio d'Agnolo but there is no decisive evidence to support this attribution.

What is known for certain is that, before the palazzo was built on this site in the sixteenth century, the fifteenth-century home of one of the most eminent Florentine Humanists, Poggio Bracciolini, stood here. That building, along with other adjoining structures, was later purchased by Giovanni del Zaccheria, who sold the estate in 1505 to Gherardo di Michele Da Cepperello. We can state with some certainty that the family of the latter decided to demolish the existing buildings with a view to constructing a single, large palazzo. If the family did so, it only preserved

ownership for a brief time, because by 1578 the estate was already a possession of the Alamanneschi family. The shifts in ownership over the centuries were intricate and tangled, but in 1650 the palazzo was purchased by the Dell'Antella family, and sold just twelve years later to Isabella Gerini, the wife of the senator Andrea da Verrazzano, a relative of the famed navigator and explorer.

Because the da Verrazzano family retained ownership longer than any other, the palazzo became generally known as Palazzo da Verrazzano. When the da Verrazzano family died out in 1819, however, the palazzo passed into the hands of the Casamorata family, and then the Parenti family.

In the end, the palazzo came into the possession of the Bargellini family, which still owns it and which has preserved and restored it with great devotion. Piero Bargellini, who served as mayor of Florence and was a respected writer, had his study in this building. He did much to preserve the artistic and historical treasures of the city.

And it was in this building that Mayor Bargellini lived though one of the saddest periods of modern Florentine history: the flood of November 4, 1966. The quarter of Santa Croce was one of the hardest hit, and Palazzo Bargellini—flooded five meters deep by the water of the Arno—long bore the signs of this catastrophe in the layers of muck and silt left behind when the water receded. Nowadays, nothing hints at the terrible flood damage, but Florence still remembers the bravery and devotion of Bargellini, the *sindaco dell'alluvione*, the mayor of the flood.

Palazzo Giugni
Via degli Alfani 48

When a merchant attained a certain level of prosperity, it was almost traditional for him to use part of his wealth to build a palazzo for himself, as if to demonstrate his success. Simone da Firenzuola was no exception to this rule. This brother of the noted writer Angelo da Firenzuola purchased a house with a garden on Via Alfani, and then, in 1565, commissioned Bartolomeo Ammannati to tear down the house and replace it with a far more prestigious building. Work must have proceeded quite quickly—in 1577 the new owners were already residing in their palazzo—and the results were worthy of note. In some ways the building showed signs of daring experimentation. Note the portal with its rusticated cornice topped by Doric features, or the elegant simplicity of the windows, in marked contrast with the complexity of the heraldic crest.

Of equal interest is the courtyard, entirely decorated in *pietra serena*, with distinctive independent loggias on the ground floor, and enclosed loggias on the *piano nobile*.

Simone da Firenzuola must have been quite happy with Ammannati's work, at least to judge from his will, drawn up in 1592. He forbade his two sons, Filippo and Angelo, to sell the palazzo, and enjoined them to pass it down to their own sons. Since Filippo and Angelo both died without heirs, however, the ownership of the estate passed to their sister Virginia, who was married to a certain Vincenzo Giugni. Upon her death in 1640 the palazzo became part of the estate of the Giugni family, one of the oldest and most glorious families in Florence.

Virginia's son, Niccolò Giugni, who was a senator and the marchese of Camporsevoli, established his home in this palazzo. He immediately undertook a number of projects designed to beautify the place, including the friezes that adorn the rooms, and the splendid basin in the garden. His descendants did even more they enlarged the building, adding a new interior wing, and created a remarkable grotto on the ground floor, designed and built by Lorenzo Migliorini, as well as a fine gallery on the second floor. This gallery was entirely decorated and frescoed; in it hung many excellent paintings, including a great number of Medici family portraits.

The estate remained in the Giugni family until 1830, when it was sold to Count Giovanni Maria della Porta and his wife, Caterina Doria Colonna. They were the first owners to do any substantial restorations. Even greater restorations were undertaken at the turn of the twentieth century by the Fraschetti family, which still owns this palazzo. The main purpose of the work undertaken was to restore the original size and appearance of the interior, with the elimination of additions that had been made over the years. As an example, consider the *salone* on the second floor, which the elimination of two partition walls restored to its original size. More recently, the rear facade, which overlooks the garden, also regained its original austere elegance. Currently, the large rooms on the second floor, with the exquisite gallery, house the Lyceum Fiorentino, a prestigious cultural institution.

Palazzo Budini Gattai

Piazza Santissima Annunziata 1

The ancient Palazzo Grifoni, now known as Palazzo Budini Gattai, is considered a major example of the last generation of historic Florentine palazzi—those built from scratch in the second half of the sixteenth century, either for court dignitaries or for the favorites of Cosimo de' Medici and Francesco I de' Medici. Erected some distance from the centre of Florence out of considerations of space, these new palazzi were meant to serve specific needs and offer elegant surroundings in which to receive guests. At the same time, they offered an opportunity for trying out new and original architectural solutions and approaches. Such was the case with Palazzo Grifoni, built between 1557 and 1563 for a wealthy court officer, Ugolino di Iacopo Grifoni, Cosimo's secretary and personal favorite, as well as the former butler of Duke Alessandro de' Medici.

Beginning in 1549, Grifoni had purchased a series of houses that once belonged to the Ricci family, set at the corner of Via dei Servi and Piazza della Santissima Annunziata. Eight years later, he entrusted the design

and construction of his new palazzo to the most renowned and fashionable architect of the time, Bartolomeo Ammannati, who was paid one hundred ducats for the job. Ammannati, who was building a number of other palazzi during the same period, developed a number of remarkable ideas in his work on Palazzo Grifoni. He built the facades entirely of uncovered brick, a radically new feature in the Florentine architectural landscape, and put large windows on the ground floor, which was quite a change from the projected openings and arcades of fifteenth-century palazzi. Also notable was the way in which he underscored the central vertical bays of both facades. In the facade overlooking Via dei Servi, he used a combination of portal, framed window on the second floor, and family escutcheon. He used the same approach in the facade overlooking the Piazza della Santissima Annunziata, coopting the third window on the ground floor, and thus reducing the importance of the secondary portal standing next to that window, used as a *porte cochère*. We should also consider Ammannati's refined and painstaking decoration of doors and windows, in perfect harmony with the rest of the facade. Lastly, he incorporated a five-arch interior loggia overlooking the rear garden, lavishly decorated with corbels carved by Ammannati himself. The architect also devoted considerable attention to the garden, perhaps to make up for the lack of an interior courtyard, a constant feature in the typology of the Florentine palazzo. Of particular note is the fountain of Venus, believed by some historians to have been carved by Ammannati himself, though others (specifically Ulrich Middeldorf) believe it to be the work of Giovanni Bandini.

By 1563, Palazzo Grifoni was largely complete, except perhaps for the third floor, which was missing what are now three rooms on the side overlooking the Piazza della Santissima Annunziata, near the Loggiato dei Serviti. This missing portion evidently prompted comments and criticism; nonetheless, it was not until the 1720s that Pietro Gaetano Grifoni decided to complete the third floor, and the facade. Pietro Gaetano Grifoni's wife, Lisabetta di Piero Capponi, renowned for her beauty and her entertaining, brought a period of renown and splendour to the palazzo, following its first one hundred fifty years of relative tranquillity. When the Grifoni family died out at the end of the eighteenth century, the palazzo

was purchased by Ferdinando Riccardi. He died in 1847, bequeathing the building to the Mannelli family, who in turn sold it to Niccolò Antinori. Finally, his heirs sold the palazzo to Leopoldo Gattai around 1890. Gattai was the owner, with his son-in-law Francesco Budini, of a major building company, which had received sizable contracts during a great urban renewal of Florence. This consisted of a number of projects undertaken in the wake of Tuscany's annexation to the kingdom of Italy, during which time Florence served as United Italy's capital for a short period. The work made the two men rich, and at the end of the nineteenth century they decided to purchase great amounts of farmland. They also purchased the palazzo on Via dei Servi. As soon as they held deed to this building, they set about restoring it; the architect Giuseppe Boccini decorated the building in the late-nineteenth-century style that still adorns it. In 1892 the monumental staircase was built and lavishly decorated by two artists, Burchi and Bargellini, who were working for Boccini. This staircase leads up to the *piano nobile*, which was also embellished with frescoes, wooden ornamentation, and a cunning blend of period furniture and various decorative arts, which can still be admired there. The floor in a hall on the second floor was painted in oils by the stucco-artist Fercini, who reproduced the pastoral canvases hanging in another hall on the *piano nobile*, executed for the Budini Gattai family by Raffaello Sorbi. The facade too was restored; the *seggetta di via*, a streetside bench, was rebuilt and the friezes, stone window-decorations, and cornices were redone as well.

The palazzo still belongs to the heirs of Leopoldo Gattai and Francesco Budini, who occupy only one wing. The rest of the building was leased for over twenty years to the Tuscan Regional Government, which used it as the headquarters of the regional council until the end of 1994.

The palazzo is now entirely available to the Budini Gattai family.

Palazzo Corsini Suarez
Via Maggio 42

In the quarter of Santo Spirito stood the earliest houses of the Corsini family, who arrived in Florence in the mid-twelfth century from the Val di Pesa. This family of hard-working merchants had established a trading company by the year 1300, and possessed considerable wealth. Even the financial downfall of Edward III, the king of England, failed to unhinge this family's great power when many of the great financiers of Florence, including the Bardi and Peruzzi families, who had extended considerable loans to the English monarch, were ruined by his insolvency.

In the fourteenth century, the houses of the Corsini family were clustered on Via Maggio. The largest of these houses belonged to Messer Filippo (1334-1421), brother of the cardinal Pietro. Filippo served as ambassador more than once, but his position of eminence ultimately led to unfortunate consequences. During the uprising of the Ciompi, a revolt against the more powerful families and the domineering rule of the Arti

Maggiori, the leading guilds, Filippo's houses were burnt, and almost all were razed to the ground. Filippo was not easily discouraged, however, and when the situation seemed to be under control, he set about rebuilding. The new palazzo that arose was an imposing building in the classical fourteenth-century style, with two rows of ample windows (still present) on the second and third floors. The facade was stern and elegant, and had six vertical bays of windows.

The palazzo was inherited by Filippo's second-born son, Gherardo, and remained the property of Gherardo's descendants until 1559. Over the following thirty years, the palazzo changed owners twice; it was first deeded to Marzio Marzi de' Medici, the bishop of Marsico; then to Matteo Bartoli. In 1590 it was purchased by a Portuguese nobleman, Baltasar Suarez de la Concha, a courtier who was related to the grand duke himself (he was married to the sister of Camilla Martelli, the second wife of Cosimo I). Along with the palazzo, Suarez purchased two adjoining houses located to the rear, on the side running parallel with Via Maggio. He then took great pains to join all three buildings, incorporating them into the single structure of the palazzo. The palazzo thus acquired a second, narrower facade overlooking Borgo Tegolaio. Suarez also enlarged the courtyard, to which decorative capitals and architraves were added.

At the beginning of the seventeenth century, Baltasar's son, Fernando, hired Gherardo Silvani, a noted architect, to make some improvements in the building. Among these improvements was probably the redone ground-floor facade, with the *inginocchiate* windows and a large central portal, and the entire fourth floor, with its slightly smaller windows, and immense jutting eaves, embellished with carved heraldic motifs. Counterbalancing those eaves on the interior is the immense wooden canopy with carved shells and spheres, which overhangs the courtyard on three sides.

The courtyard is quite interesting in and of itself. Note the balcony that runs around the entire second floor, and the unusual octagonal fourteenth-century pillars. These latter were the source of inspiration for later capitals and columns installed during the ownership of the Suarez family, and feature the Suarez coat-of-arms, along with the Cross of St. Stephen. The Suarez family was endowed with the Baliato di Firenze, the highest ranking title of the Order of the Knights of St. Stephen, and since

the palazzo, as part of the family estate, automatically became part of the Baliato di Firenze, it was for many years generally called the Palazzo della Commenda di Firenze.

When the Suarez family died out, the palazzo on Via Maggio became city property, and was used as the headquarters of a branch of the Florentine police force. The first restoration dates from 1918 and was financed by the city of Florence. More thoroughgoing restorations were done in the 1970s, when the city government decided to make the building the headquarters of the Archivio Contemporaneo del Gabinetto Scientifico Letterario G.P. Vieusseux, one of the most respected cultural institutions of Florence, long headed by Alessandro Bonsanti, an intellectual and a former mayor, who has lavished care and dedication upon it.

Established in 1979 and opened to the public many years later, the Archivio, a scholarly archive of literature, possesses major collections donated by leading figures of nineteenth- and twentieth-century Italian culture (among them, Giuseppe Montanelli, Emilio Cecchi, Angiolo Orvieto, Giuseppe De Robertis, Eugenio Montale, and Alessandro Bonsanti himself). It is now one of the most important cultural centres in the Oltrarno area. In the 1990s, the ground floor became the offices of the Gabinetto di Restauro Librario (Studio for the Restoration of Books), which was an offshoot of the Gabinetto Vieusseux, founded directly following the disastrous flood of 1966. It was founded to rescue the books in the library run by the Gabinetto in Palazzo Strozzi—books that were badly damaged by the mixture of mud and fuel-oil carried by the flood waters. Thousands of volumes have indeed been saved through the work of this virtually unique centre, which operated for twenty years in the rooms of the Certosa Cistercense del Galluzzo (Cistercian Charter House). And many more books will be rescued in the future (among them books from the Biblioteca Nazionale Centrale in Florence, Italy's national library) in the new and permanent offices on Via Maggio.

Palazzo Ricasoli Firidolfi
Via Maggio 7

One of the chief thoroughfares in the densely inhabited quarter of Oltrarno is Via Maggio. While the name might suggest a reference to the month of May (*maggio*), it is in fact a reference to *maggiore*, or "largest," because this has long been the quarter's main street. It should therefore come as little surprise that some of the most prestigious and remarkable palazzi in Santo Spirito line this street in particular.

Palazzo Ricasoli Firidolfi was built by the Ridolfi family, not, as the name would suggest, the Ricasoli family. The Ridolfi, at the turn of the sixteenth century, acquired a number of houses on this street, houses which had previously belonged to the Velluti and the Migliori families. Then senator Giovanni Francesco Ridolfi had those houses demolished in order to build his own palazzo in their place. Around 1530 he took up residence in the new palazzo with his wife, Camilla Pandolfini. The children and descendants of the couple distinguished themselves for their generous

commitment to public life and politics, as well as for their love of the arts. Before long, in fact, the palazzo contained a number of fine sculptures and paintings.

When this branch of the family died out in the seventeenth century, however, their entire estate fell into the hands of another Ridolfi branch, descendants of Piero Ridolfi and Contessina de' Medici, one of the daughters of Lorenzo the Magnificent. It remained in their possession until they sold it to Maria Lucrezia Firidolfi in 1756. Firidolfi was a new surname adopted by a branch of the Ricasoli family, and over the decades, and through a series of marriages, the various lines of this family were reconnected. Lucrezia Firidolfi married Giovanni Francesco Ricasoli Zanchini, then their son Alberto married Elisabetta Ricasoli, the sole heir to Bettino Ricasoli, until the palazzo was rightly given the name of Ricasoli.

Over time the Ricasoli family also established ties with the Corsini and the Rosselli Del Turco families, and they continued to live in their home on Via Maggio until the early decades of the twentieth century. The Ricasoli family certainly rivalled the Ridolfi family's love for culture and the arts. Their library became famous, and their collection of art was equally renowned, featuring paintings by Fra Bartolommeo and Caravaggio. The halls and the *salone* (great hall) had been frescoed in high style during the eighteenth and nineteenth centuries. Of special note was the chapel, which is traditionally said to have been decorated by Giorgio Vasari himself. As for the designer and builder of the palazzo as a whole, the name remains unknown. We do know that the facade originally had no windows on the ground floor. The handsome *inginocchiate* windows were added only in a later phase.

The courtyard, on the other hand, is intact in its original form. It has a simple, soaring elegance, with a stern portico that is softened by exquisite capitals and corbels, decorated with alternating Ridolfi family crests and images of St. John the Baptist, patron saint of the first owner of the palazzo, Giovanni Francesco Ridolfi. Also intact is the steep stairway with stone decoration that leads up to the *piano nobile*, whose entry vestibule also maintains its fifteenth-century appearance and layout.

The profusion of frescoes adorning the halls are based on Biblical and mythological themes, and are clearly eighteenth-century in style. The

frescoes in the large *salone*, on the other hand, date from the nineteenth century.
If we can still today admire the features of this palazzo in all their beauty, the credit goes in part to the farsighted initiative of Baron Alberto Ricasoli Firidolfi, who spent heavily in the second half of the nineteenth century to restore the exterior of the palazzo. More recently, restorations have been done, chiefly inside, on the frescoes that adorn the halls.
The palazzo is still property of the Ricasoli family, but is now occupied by a dance school.

Palazzo Rosselli Del Turco
Borgo Santi Apostoli 17

One of the few Romanesque churches in Florence, the lovely church of the Santi Apostoli in the little Piazzetta del Limbo, is interesting but relatively little-known. Located along the narrow Borgo Santi Apostoli, the *piazzetta* is so-named because a children's cemetery was once located there. (Catholics believe unbaptized children spend eternity in Limbo). The little church hardly stands out among the tall buildings that surround it, and it was even more overshadowed four centuries ago when an impressive, aristocratic villa rose by its side.

It was the turn of the sixteenth century, and the Borgherini were a particularly well-to-do family. Because they owned a number of houses along the Borgo Santi Apostoli, directly adjoining the church, they hired the esteemed architect Baccio d'Agnolo to build a palazzo worthy of their high estate. The chief client was Salvi Borgherini, and we know that in 1515 the palazzo must already have been completed, or at least suitable for habitation, because in that year Salvi's son Pierfrancesco Borgherini

was married to Margherita Acciaiuoli. The dowry of walnut furniture and other objects that her father ordered from Baccio d'Agnolo became legendary. There were chests, chest-benches, headboards, and beds, all finely carved and painted, and all meant to decorate the halls of the palazzo. So great was their fame that, during the siege of Florence in 1530 by the king of France, the Florentine Republic seriously contemplated offering the whole set of furniture to the royal besieger, in hope of placating his wrath. Only Margherita's vociferous protests (Pierfrancesco was in exile at the time) prevented the cowed Florentine government from doing so.

Baccio d'Agnolo had started work on the building in 1507, and was immediately faced with specific obstacles. The nearby church considerably limited the available space, and all decisions had to take the church into account, since the south side of the palazzo joined its perimeter.

One of the first and most notable obstacles was lack of space for a courtyard. Thus, the courtyard was replaced by an atrium directly adjoining the presbytery and apse of the church. From that atrium ran the two-part staircase that led up to the entry foyer on the *piano nobile*. Two more flights of this staircase, which led up to the third floor, have since been partially demolished and rebuilt. In a curious use of materials, the ceiling above the stairway was constructed entirely of stone.

On the second floor is the *salone*, a notably handsome room in which Benedetto da Rovezzano, who had at the time (1505) just returned from France, built an elegant fireplace entirely decorated with bas-reliefs. It is now in the Museo del Bargello. He built another solemn and linear fireplace for an adjoining room, which is thought to be the bedroom of Pierfrancesco and Margherita. The wooden *solai* (ceilings) are also quite interesting—they were built by a team of master woodworkers and specialized craftsmen who worked with Baccio d'Agnolo. This same team also made all of the doors and the nail-studded shutters on the windows. Baccio completed his work with a three-light *altana*, a covered roof-terrace facing south and overlooking the church of Santi Apostoli.

Around 1530 Pierfrancesco Borgherini and his brother Giovanni purchased a number of houses across from the palazzo. They intended to use the land to lay out the garden that was in such fashionable demand at the time, and which could be created in no other way. A small, verdant

appendage was thus established, separated from the palazzo itself by the Borgo Santi Apostoli.

The palazzo remained in the Borgherini family until 1749 when Senator Pier Francesco Borgherini was overwhelmed by massive debt. Two findings against him by bankruptcy court led to the confiscation of the palazzo by the Uffizio dell'Abbondanza. In order to pay off Borgherini's creditors, the palazzo was sold to the brothers Giovan Antonio, Stefano, and Girolamo di Chiarissimo Rosselli Del Turco, at a price of 7,564 florins. This family still owns the palazzo.

Beginning in the middle of the nineteenth century, the first structural modifications were made. Giovan Battista, son of the marchese Luigi Rosselli Del Turco, had a belvedere built, along with the long terrace high atop the roof. Following the death of Giovan Battista Rosselli Del Turco in 1865, the estate was inherited by his brother, Vincenzo, a canon, and it was he who had a second portal built to the left of the main one. This was done with the division of the interior in mind, so that apartments could be rented separately, as was common practice at that time. When Vincenzo died in 1891, his nephew Antonio once again occupied the entire *piano nobile* himself. It was Antonio who had the main *salone* split up, creating two spectacular little parlors in period style, which were later lavishly furnished.

The palazzo is still split internally, and this has allowed it to be used for numerous purposes. The owners still reside on the top floor, while the second floor houses a renowned Italian fashion group.

Palazzo Ginori
Via dei Ginori 11

The Ginori family made their fortune in the lucrative trade of banking, and invested more than once in real estate in the quarter of San Lorenzo, where they lived not far from the old basilica of San Lorenzo. At the turn of the sixteenth century, the leading member in this family was Carlo di Lionardo Ginori, who distinguished himself by his competent efforts in more than one public office, and by his marked predilection for patronage of the arts (he liked to surround himself with artists and writers, and among his many protégés was Andrea del Sarto).

Carlo di Lionardo Ginori paid 1,500 florins in 1515 for a house and two small *casette*, which had belonged to the Ubaldini da Pesciola until that family died out. These buildings were also located in the section of Borgo San Lorenzo that was later known as Via Ginori. Beginning in 1516 Carlo di Lionardo Ginori had these buildings demolished, to make way for the fine palazzo that he intended to construct for himself.

Baccio d'Agnolo was one of the many artists who moved in the circle of Carlo di Lionardo Ginori. We know that Baccio was summoned at one point to arbitrate a dispute concerning boundaries of the property upon

which the palazzo was being erected. We further know that Baccio was commissioned by Carlo Ginori to do a number of pieces for the Villa di Torre di Baroncoli, near Calenzano, the Ginoris' home town, from which they had moved to Florence at the end of the thirteenth century. For these reasons, and because of the appearance of a number of elements in the facade and the courtyard, several scholars have identified the palazzo on what is now Via Ginori as a creation of Baccio d'Agnolo.

Plausible though it may be, this hypothesis is not supported by any direct evidence. It is also impossible to ignore the great number of similarities between this palazzo and the one on Via dei Servi, property of the Niccolini family, and attributed with certainty to Domenico d'Agnolo, Baccio's son who was also an architect.

Built between 1516 and 1520, the new home was particularly impressive, towering over the other houses that lined the streets of the quarter. It stood three stories tall, and was crowned by a loggia. There were six vertical bays of windows and an off-centre portal in line with the fourth bay, flanked by five little rectangular windows on the ground floor and a distinctive *panca di via* (streetside bench) that was removed in the nineteenth century. The entire building showed a marked upward thrust in its design, counterbalanced by the sharply projecting eaves.

The courtyard, which was porticoed on four sides, was exquisitely adorned with fine capitals and brackets. When Carlo Ginori died in 1527, the palazzo was inherited by his nephew Lionardo, who married Caterina di Tommaso Soderini, a woman who was renowned for her great love of the arts. She was also notorious as the aunt of Lorenzino de' Medici, the son of Pierfrancesco and Maria Soderini. Lorenzino dangled the bait of an amorous encounter with Caterina to lure Duke Alessandro de' Medici into his palazzo, where he was ambushed and murdered. Since that time, the *casa principale* of the Ginori family has remained the property of the descendents of Lionardo and Caterina, and has undergone a number of substantial changes.

Between 1691 and 1701 the palazzo was enlarged under the supervision of the architect Lorenzo Merlini to take advantage of a small house with garden on Via della Stufa that had been acquired by the Ginori. Merlini built a complex that enclosed the small garden and fountain on three

sides, with a balustraded terrace on the second floor. Inside, the reception hails were lavishly frescoed and decorated by Antonio Ferri, Alessandro Gherardini, and Gian Domenico Ferretti.

The decades that followed saw a further expansion, with the purchase of an adjoining house that had once belonged to Baccio Bandinelli, and a thoroughgoing renovation of the furnishings in order to live up to the Palazzo's new social reputation. Other work was done under the supervision of the engineer Felice Francolini in the mid-nineteenth century, when the palazzo belonged to the marchese Lorenzo Ginori Lisci, a member of a branch of the Ginori family.

Lorenzo had the palazzo paved in marble, enclosed the courtyard with a cast-iron and glass skylight, and built a broad, handsome stairway, to replace the steep original staircase.

Since then, the palazzo has undergone nothing more serious than changes in the furnishings and decorations, in accordance with the tastes of various eras. And at the end of the nineteenth century, during the lifetime of the many-faceted marchese Carlo Benedetto Ginori, the second-story *salone* was the site of a celebrated and popular five-year series of literary conferences, organized by the marchese himself.

The palazzo still belongs to the Ginori Lisci family, which resides there.

Palazzo Niccolini

Via dei Servi 15

Between 1548 and 1550, Bastiano Ciaini da Montauto, a noted and wealthy merchant, engaged the services of Domenico d'Agnolo, a renowned architect and woodworker, and the son of Baccio d'Agnolo. Bastiano asked Domenico to build him a fitting palazzo on the street that then ran straight toward the square on which fronts the sanctuary of the Santissima Annunziata (Our Lady of the Holy Annunciation). And Domenico, clearly wishing to erect a well proportioned, tall building, took clear inspiration—one might say total inspiration—from the palazzo of the Marchesi Ginori, which many consider to have been designed by Baccio d'Agnolo. The resulting facade was nearly identical to that of its model and inspiration, with a streetside bench, and rectangular windows on the ground floor. The courtyard is considerably more original; it is porticoed on four sides, each side partitioned into three arches. The upper two floors are rendered even taller by the elegant architraved windows, surmounted by stringcourse cornices and a series of oculi.

Over time the rear facade proved to be more striking still. It overlooks the garden, and was embellished with two graceful loggias; one corresponding to the ground floor, the other to the second floor.

By the time these loggias were built, however, the palazzo had a new owner. In fact, Bastiano da Montauto had engendered a great many daughters, but had no son to serve as heir. When Bastiano died, therefore, the entire estate passed over to his nephew, Benedetto, the son of Bastiano's brother Matteo. In order to get out of a financial scrape, Benedetto was forced to sell all his real estate, and the palazzo on Via dei Servi was purchased by Giovanni di Agnolo Niccolini, of an ancient and aristocratic family that had given more than one leading citizen to the Florentine Republic.

Giovanni Niccolini was a senator, and was dedicated to the law, like many in his family. He lived in Rome for many years as an ambassador; at the same time he sponsored the construction of a family chapel in the church of Santa Croce, designed and built by Giovanni Antonio Dosio. Dosio often worked for Niccolini—so often that for a certain period of time he

lived in the palazzo itself. It seems quite likely that he designed the ground-floor loggia of the rear facade. Giovanni Niccolini also embellished his Florentine home with fine works of art and Roman antiquities. Giovanni's son, Filippo Niccolini, oversaw the construction of the second-floor loggia on the rear facade at the turn of the seventeenth century; moreover he was responsible for commissioning, over the course of three decades, most of the frescoes that decorate the halls. This project was carried forward by a series of noted artists: the Volterrano, Giacinto Gemignani, Angelo Michele Colonna (who created the entire decorative array of the gallery), Jacopo Chiavistelli, and Antonio Ciseri. Because Filippo died in 1666 without male offspring, his palazzo became the inheritance of the senator Lorenzo Niccolini, from a collateral branch of the Niccolini di Camugliano. This branch of the family, in turn, was forced to sell the palazzo through a remarkable bureaucratic imbroglio having to do with the inheritance laws; this, after they had paid for futher painting of rooms during the course of the eighteenth century. They sold it in 1824 to Count Dmitri Bouturline, counsellor of the Tsar, and an impassioned bibliophile.

While part of the quarters in the palazzo were rented out, others were prepared to accommodate the collection of venerable old books belonging to the new owner. During this period, the garden was rearranged, and the facade overlooking Via dei Servi was decorated in graffiti and frescoes. This was done by a number of artists, including Bandinelli, Valtancoli, Sarti, and Zucconi. In 1918—the year after the Russian Revolution—the Bouturline family sold the palazzo to the Pinucci family. Eleven years later, that family sold it to the Federazione dei Fasci di Combattimento di Firenze, a Fascist veteran's organization; the palazzo served as headquarters for the organization for many years. With the fall of Fascism, the building became the property of the Ministero dei Lavori Pubblici (Italian Ministry for Public Works), which still owns it. At the end of the 1950s, the ministry undertook a massive restoration and reorganization of the palazzo to recover its original architectural lines and splendid painted decorations.

Palazzo Pucci
Via dei Pucci 6

The large palazzo that occupies much of Via dei Pucci—and which, in terms of size, length, and number of windows, seems to be one of the most impressive buildings in Florence—has only acquired these features in the relatively recent past. For many years it was nothing more than a *casa*, and not a palazzo at all.

The Pucci came to Florence from the country in the thirteenth century, and quickly acquired a prestigious reputation that was clearly endorsed by the numerous public offices that family members were summoned to fill. One of the factors that clearly encouraged their rise in favour was their steady adherence to the Medici family. Puccio Pucci was one of the most determined leaders of the pro-Medici faction during the lifetime of Cosimo the Elder; when Cosimo was exiled from Florence, Puccio openly worked to bring him quickly back. When the situation changed in Cosimo's favor, he rewarded Puccio generously. At this time (in the early fifteenth century), the Pucci family was already split into two main branches, one headed by Puccio, the other by his brother Saracino.

Puccio Pucci possessed a number of houses in the area now occupied by Via dei Servi, not far from the Ospedale di Santa Maria Nuova. His descendants continued to live in those houses, and carried on his proMedici policies, at times taking them to extremes. Giannozzo, a nephew of Puccio, was in fact beheaded for plotting to bring Pietro II the Unfortunate back to Florence during the second exile of the Medici.

Around 1450, Puccio's son Antonio purchased the group of houses, including *piazza* and vegetable garden, that can fairly be considered the core of the future palazzo.

Meanwhile, the family's power was waxing constantly: the Pucci family had established ties with Pope Paul III Farnese, and by the turn of the sixteenth century, boasted a number of senators and no fewer than three cardinals.

One of those cardinals, Roberto Pucci, was the fifth son of Antonio di Puccio. Before setting out in his ecclesiastical career, Roberto had been married to a daughter of the historian Francesco Guicciardini. She had

borne him a son named Pandolfo. This son "distinguished" himself by coming up with a plot against the grand duke Cosimo I (the first Pucci to turn against the Medici!) and was hanged.

His son, Orazio, was determined to avenge his father's death, and he too wound up on the gallows, under Francesco I.

This rash behaviour led to the confiscation of all the Pucci family's possessions, a harsh judgement that was overruled by the grand duke himself, who was aware of the merit the family had shown over the years.

In the very years in which these decisions were being made, the Pucci family began to enlarge their chief home. This home, upon the death of Lorenzo di Antonio in 1531, had become the property of his brother, Roberto, and was subsequently inherited by Roberto's children, who spent immense sums to decorate and improve it.

This building must have corresponded roughly to the central section of the present-day palazzo, which indeed stands out for its particularly exquisite architectural composition and its decorations. In addition, there were the houses on either side, which remained distinct and separate.

When the Puccio branch of the family died out in 1612, the entire estate was inherited by the heirs of Saracino, specifically the senator Niccolò Pucci. Thanks to the separate buildings, when Niccolò died, his sons were able to break up the inheritance with relative ease: Giulio received the central palazzo, while Alessandro received the houses on the corner of Via dei Servi.

Giulio's son, Orazio Pucci, purchased a number of houses that stood on the other side of his property, and in 1688 he asked Paolo Falconieri to unify all of the facades to go with the facade of the central structure. And because Giulio's heirs did much the same thing at the turn of the eighteenth century, it finally became possible to speak of a true Palazzo Pucci.

The palazzo, however, has remained split into two parts. There is the larger half, which includes the nucleus of the entire complex, once the property of the Pucci di Barsento branch of the family. This half still has the two courtyards of the two core residential structures that it originally comprised. The halls in this half were richly frescoed in the eighteenth century by Giuseppe Bezzuoli and Luigi Ademollo. The ballroom was

decorated with stuccoes, which were redone at the behest of the senator Orazio Roberto Pucci at the end of the eighteenth century. Lastly, the recent addition of a "roadway" runs through entranceways and court-yards, and provides a handy way into the groundfloor rooms.

This part of the palazzo was split up in this century between the two sons of the Marchese Emilio Pucci. It is safe to say that, despite a renovation here and there, the building boasts an excellent state of preservation.

The other portion of the large building, which overlooks Via dei Servi, has both its own entrance and its own courtyard, as well as a set of notable frescoes by Giovanni da San Giovanni occupying a few of the halls. After a series of owners, the palazzo wound up in the hands of the Mensa Arcivescovile di Firenze (Dining Hall of the Archbishops, Florence). It is still owned by the local Curia of the Roman Catholic Church.

Among the more notable facts concerning this palazzo is that the well known Circolo Artistico, one of the leading artistic organizations in this city, had its headquarters here between 1887 and 1888. All of the lead-ing painters of the Macchiaioli school frequented this building. Indeed, the inauguration of the Circolo Artistico in Palazzo Pucci was presided over by no less a personage than Margherita of Savoy, queen of Italy.

Finally, there is an odd bit of history surrounding a window that has been bricked up at the corner of Via dei Servi. It is said that one of the con-spiring henchmen of Pandolfo Pucci crept out this window on his way to attempt to assassinate Cosimo I.

Palazzo Corsini in Parione
Via del Parione 11/12

There is a palazzo in Florence that has its main entrance on Via del Parione, yet it overlooks the banks of the river Arno with an impressively long balcony and a thoroughly distinctive appearance. Indeed, the riverfront facade has very few of the features normally found in the more classical homes of the Florentine aristocracy. This is the palazzo of the Corsini family. In terms of the time of its construction and its overall appearance, this palazzo fits into none of the Florentine architectural categories examined thus far. In fact, it is far more similar in typology to the palazzo found in Rome. It has many links to the Palazzo di Gino Capponi, which is treated later in this book.

On this site in the sixteenth century stood the houses of Bindo Altoviti, a wealthy banker and celebrated patron of the arts who lived in Rome for many years. He opposed the designs of the Medici with such persistence that he was declared a rebellious outlaw by Cosimo I. His property was seized and his houses were assigned to Don Giovanni.

Don Giovanni added new purchases to his estate, had the houses decorated, and surrounded them with gardens, creating a sort of country lodge, in the midst of the city. Here he loved to gather his friends and hold sumptuous banquets. After his death in 1621, the property passed to Don Lorenzo de' Medici, the son of Ferdinand I, who showed the same predilection for hosting banquets. Particularly notorious was the huge banquet he hosted in 1630 in honour of the members of the Accademia della Crusca, a learned society. A detailed and astonished description of

it survives in the letters of Francesco Redi. When Don Lorenzo died, the Medici decided to sell off the entire complex; in 1640, it was purchased for the sum of 14,150 *scudi*, coins of the grand duchy, by Maddalena Machiavelli, widow of a Corsini, who immediately deeded it to her eighteen-year-old son, the marchese Bartolommeo Corsini. It was he who set about the radical project of renovation that was soon to transform the appearance of the palazzo.

In 1650, the architect Alfonso Parigi the Younger was assigned to undertake the restoration of the original *casino*. Then Bartolommeo Corsini asked Ferdinando Tacca—son of the betterknown Pietro Tacca—to enlarge the building. He built the impressive facade overlooking Via del Parione, with twenty-three vertical bays of windows. This facade may have been based on designs by Alfonso Parigi.

Work continued at a good clip until 1671, when a series of interruptions ensued. Despite them, an elegant spiral staircase was built by Pier Francesco Silvani. When the marchese Bartolommeo Corsini died in 1685, his son and heir, Filippo, cracked the whip. Work began again in earnest: in 1686 he obtained permission to build a long balcony overlooking the banks of the Arno. It was designed and built by the architect Antonio Ferri, as were the elevations overlooking the courtyard. Following this, work went forward, respectively, on the new second-floor *salone* (main hall); on the monumental staircase (1694-1695); and, lastly, on the remarkable grotto on the ground floor. During this same period (1695-1700) the rooms and halls in the wing of the palazzo extending toward Ponte a Santa Trinita were frescoed. Antonio Domenico Gabbiani did the *salone* and the gallery overlooking the Arno; Piero Dandini did the rooms overlooking Via del Parione; and Tommaso Gherardini did the bedroom, with the halls of Ceres and the Arts. Under Filippo's son, named Bartolommeo like his grandfather, all work was finally completed. The young Bartolommeo oversaw the completion of the wing of the palazzo extending toward Ponte alla Carraia. Once that wing was complete, the facade overlooking the Arno gained the distinctive baroque appearance—in many ways exquisitely Roman—that aroused such perplexity among the Florentines. The central structure, on a line with the courtyard, was sharply recessed, and the two wings were surmounted by

statues—none of which was in tune with the architecture of the city or prevailing tastes. Still, the whole structure was soon accepted as a remarkably striking piece of architecture.

The palazzo, then, was definitively completed in 1735. In the same general period, a Corsini had been made pope, as Clement XII; this was Lorenzo Corsini, the brother of the same Filippo who had done so much to build this new palazzo.

As if to pronounce good the splendid new palazzo, the pope sent a statue of himself to Florence, and Girolamo Ticciati decided to place it on the first landing of the monumental staircase. This was done in 1737.

From that time on, the palazzo was the site of continual entertaining and receiving, especially during the time of the prince, Lorenzo, who was the Grand Prior of Pisa of the Order of Malta, thanks to the benevolent interest of his great-uncle the pope. Lorenzo gave memorable feasts and parties; he loved to surround himself with artists, and filled his court with them. When French troops arrived in Florence at the end of the eigh-

teenth century, the elderly prince chose to take refuge in Vienna. His palazzo thus came to be the new home of General Murat and his family; later it became the meeting place of the most determined supporters of Elisa Baciocchi, Napoleon Bonaparte's sister. When the grand duke returned to the city, the palazzo enjoyed a new moment of splendour in 1870 when, at the order of the new king, Victor Emmanuel II of Savoy, its halls were used for the official reception of the delegation that had come from Madrid to offer the Spanish crown to Prince Amadeus of Aosta. Moreover, at the behest of the Prince Tommaso, until the early years of the twentieth century, the palazzo continued to host a great annual ball, to which all the chief authorities of the city were invited.

The palazzo still belongs to the Corsini family. During the twentieth century the family has been faced with two catastrophic events. In 1944 German explosives damaged the structure of the palazzo, and in 1966 the terrible flood of the river Arno devastated the ground floor and the basement, including the remarkable grotto. The damage was soon repaired, and in time the building was restored to its former splendour. Visitors can still admire the halls of the gallery, containing the leading private art collection in Florence, and in a well-ventilated attic, one of Florence's leading painters, Luciano Guarnieri, has established his studio.

Palazzo Portinari Salviati
Via del Corso 6

Along the Corso, one of the main streets of early Florence, the names and histories of two families were bound up with one another, and became famous.

Along this street, as early as the thirteenth century, the Portinari family owned a number of houses. The Portinari were well-to-do bankers, and over the course of the fifteenth century, many of the Portinari were partners in or served as officers of the Banco Mediceo di Milano or the Banco Mediceo di Bruges. (One of them, Folco Portinari, was traditionally said to have been the father of Dante's Beatrice). Moreover, they had close ties with the great architect Michelozzo. It is not unreasonable to think that they asked Michelozzo to design the great palazzo that was to replace their several houses in the Corso.

Tommaso Portinari, in particular, was known throughout the business world of Europe. It seems that he may have paid for the first phase of construction in the area surrounding the courtyard; he may also have been behind the construction of a unified facade, when the composite building first attained a clear physiognomy.

Over the course of the sixteenth century, the fortunes of the Portinari family declined steadily. They were forced to sell off the houses along the Corso, one by one, to another family whose fortunes were steadily improving: the Salviati.

The Salviati family had been particularly prominent in the time of the Florentine Republic, and had produced many leading citizens, sixty-three Priori (heads of guilds), and twenty-one Gonfalonieri (rulers of Florence). The family reputation gained great luster when Iacopo di Giovanni Salviati married one of the daughters of Lorenzo the Magnificent— Lucrezia de' Medici—followed by the otherwise unhappy marriage between Maria Salviati and Giovanni dalle Bande Nere, which did however produce Cosimo, the future first grand duke of Tuscany.

As early as the beginning of the sixteenth century, the Salviati began to purchase the houses along the Corso that belonged to the Portinari, and in 1546 they received the deed to the new palazzo. The first family mem-

ber to own it was Iacopo di Alamanno, first cousin of Cosimo, the new grand duke. Nearly thirty years after purchasing it, spanning the years between 1572 and 1578, Iacopo carried out a great series of decorative improvements. He had a garden installed behind the palazzo, and enclosed the garden with a loggia; he built a little chapel, and a lovely courtyard. The courtyard was later known as the Cortile degli Imperatori (Courtyard of the Emperors); it was completely frescoed by Alessandro Allori (with assistants). Allori also painted a number of canvases that were hung in the many halls of the palazzo. He was a renowned architect, and had been appointed to replace Bartolomeo Ammannati as the director of construction of the Opera del Duomo (as the cathedral, Santa Maria del Fiore, was officially called while under construction). It is likely that Allori built other sections of the palazzo, but no documents have survived to prove this. There are even scholars who claim that Ammannati worked on Palazzo Portinari at some point, though again this is without evidence. We do know that the twelve busts of Roman emperors distributed throughout the courtyard in niches were purchased in Venice in 1575.

At the end of the seventeenth century, the palazzo and the facade on the left side were enlarged in order to make room for the increasingly demanding social life of the inhabitants (the spectacular entertaining that was done here lived on in Florentine memory); carriages were thus afforded easier entrance as well.

The eighteenth century began with a memorable gala held to honour twenty-seven members of the Accademia della Crusca, a learned society, on the evening of September 18, 1701. The evening culminated in an elaborate banquet, held in the loggia surrounding the courtyard.

If the century began gloriously, it continued with the extinction of the main branch of the Salviati family in 1704. As a result the palazzo passed into the hands of a branch of the family, that descended from Antonio, son of the senator Filippo.

The new owners were in time to offer fitting hospitality to the king of Denmark, Frederick Augustus IV, in 1708, under legendary circumstances. When the Danish sovereign was a young prince and the heir apparent, he had traveled to Italy, and visited Lucca. There he met a young noblewoman of the Dei Trenta family. Love blossomed between

them, but for dynastic reasons, that love could not be sanctioned by marriage. The heir apparent returned to Denmark, abandoning the young girl. She, in despair, decided to become a nun. Once he became king, Frederick Augustus returned to Florence, expressly to see the woman he had loved years before. Because she was in a cloistered convent, it was quite difficult to obtain permission to see her, but in the end he won out. They met in the Florentine convent of Santa Maria Maddalena de' Pazzi. The two former lovers spoke at length in the presence of another nun. All that is known of their conversation is that the young woman tried more than once to persuade Frederick Augustus to convert to Roman Catholicism.

The shift in ownership at the turn of the eighteenth century marked a new direction in the fate of the palazzo. As the decades passed, the steady application of matrimonial politics loosened the bonds between the Salviati and the city of Florence, and strengthened their ties to Rome. In 1768, following the marriage of the last descendant of the family, Anna Maria Luisa Salviati, to Prince Marc'Antonio Borghese, the palazzo was sold to Niccolò Serguidi. It was Serguidi who paid for the decoration of the halls on the second floor and the gallery. We know that the palazzo belonged to the Da Cepperello family in 1816, that it became property of the state in 1865, and that it was used as the main office of the Ministry of Justice. In 1870 it became property of the city of Florence, and later the Cassa di Risparmio di Firenze. In 1881 itbecamepropertyof the Padri Scolopi, a religious order, and for many years they ran their religious schools in the palazzo. Finally, in 1921, the bank Credito Toscano purchased the original home of the Portinari to make it into the main office of the Banca Toscana, which it remains. The Banca Toscana financed extensive restoration, rehung the paintings by Alessandro Allori, and restored an enormous apartment on the second floor for entertaining and receptions. A number of rooms now display the art collection that the bank has assembled over the years.

Palazzo di Gino Capponi
Via Gino Capponi 26

The palazzi of Florence—with all their typological and chronological variations—tend to present a relatively repetitive, conventional appearance. It is thus fairly easy to identify the typical Florentine palazzo.

There is one building, however, of comparatively recent vintage (dating from the eighteenth century), set close to the great ring roads, and only a short distance away from the Palazzo Della Gherardesca—that does not quite fit in. This building was clearly inspired, in size, splendour, and design, by the Roman palazzi of the time. The building is known as the Palazzo di Gino Capponi, although the man who actually ordered it built

was the senator Alessandro Capponi. Capponi was a member of an illustrious and aristocratic Florentine family, with venerable historical roots; among its forefathers was the renowned Florentine patriot Pier Capponi, who courageously led the defense of the city against the troops of Charles VIII, King of France, who invaded Italy in 1495-1496.

The Capponi were one of the oldest and noblest families in Florence (and, as we have seen, they already owned the so-called Palazzo Capponi delle Rovinate on Via de' Bardi). In the eighteenth century, moreover, they were also quite wealthy, thanks to their profitable activities in business and trade. Senator Alessandro Capponi, who lived between the late-seventeenth and early-eighteenth centuries, was one of the leading figures in Roman high society. When he returned to Florence in 1699 and married

the noblewoman Bianca Ricasoli, it seems he felt a need to build a fragment of the Eternal City in the city of his forefathers. He purchased—from Duke Anton Maria Salviati, a direct descendant of Lorenzo the Magnificent by the female line—the huge estate that had thus far been handed down from father to son in the Medici family. Set just beyond the church of the Santissima Annunziata, the estate possessed a lovely little country lodge, and featured renowned plantations of rare and exotic plants. It was valued at about 12,000 *scudi*, a coin of the time.

The new owner immediately ordered that his new property be surveyed, and that accurate maps be drawn up. In spring of 1702 he ordered these maps sent to Rome, to the architect Carlo Fontana, and asked Fontana to make plans for the construction of an impressive new palazzo.

In August of the same year, in exchange for the sizable fee of 85 *scudi*, Fontana sent plans and a drawing of the new palazzo. An engineer named Alessandro Cecchini immediately set about building it. Construction began with the foundations and the walls of the central structure. As early as the beginning of 1704, it could be said that the central wing was complete up to the fourth floor.

The *salone*, or great hall of the *piano nobile*, however, was not finished quite so speedily; the ceiling was not completed until the end of 1706. This was to be the largest *salone* in all of Florence.

Likewise, the immense staircase was not really finished until 1708; with it, the distinctive aviary was completed. This remarkable structure, decorated with a seashell motif, stood on the left side of the garden.

Overlooking the vast garden is the secondary facade, with the two side wings set forward with respect to the central wing. This facade is actually more distinctive and noteworthy than the main facade. Indeed, the main facade is fairly monotonous, with its nineteen vertical bays of windows; it was completed in a second phase, with a small balcony, the Capponi coat-of-arms, and a stone cornice surrounding the main portal.

By 1710 work on the palazzo was complete; between 1703 and 1704 artists including Atanasio Bimbacci, Cinqui, and Camillo Sagrestani had frescoed most of the rooms.

Alessandro Capponi died in 1716, leaving his estate to his two sons, Scipione and Francesco Maria. They lived in the palazzo, and entertained in

it lavishly and often. They spent heavily to furnish it in a fitting manner. The Capponi palace, with its monumental staircase lined with statues and fountains, its galleries of paintings, and its impressive series of frescoes, soon became an attraction, drawing illustrious visitors from all over Europe. At the end of the eighteenth century, with the death of Marchese Alessandro Maria Capponi, the main branch of the family dwindled to a close. The palazzo was passed over to a secondary branch of the family; the marchese Pier Roberto Capponi left the palazzo to his son Gino, who became a leading personality in nineteenth-century Florence. A man of great learning and intellect, Gino Capponi served as president of the Accademia Colombaria. He wrote, with Pietro Vieusseux, his celebrated *Antologia*. Gino Capponi traveled extensively throughout Europe; he was friends with such major cultural figures as the poet Ugo Foscolo and the writer and statesman Chateaubriand. He transformed his Florentine palazzo into a gathering spot for leading figures in European culture. His home was graced by the presence of the great writers Alessandro Manzoni and Giacomo Leopardi, the poet and satirist Giuseppe Giusti, the poet, historian, and statesman Alphonse de Lamartine, and the politicians and writers Massimo D'Azeglio and Pietro Colletta.

When the marchese Gino Capponi died in 1876, the palazzo and its grounds were inherited by his eldest daughter Marianna, and her husband, the Genoan marchese Gentile Farinola; his family owned the palazzo until 1920.

During these years, the new owners renovated the halls of the huge residence, transforming them into independent suites of apartments. These were rented out to various families, including the Balduino family of Genoa, who were renowned for their princely entertaining.

The palazzo was then purchased by Egisto Fabbri, a wealthy Italian-American businessman, who installed his art collection there. The building was then sold to Italian Senator Alessandro Contini Bonacossi, who hung his own collection of paintings. The Palazzo still belongs to the heirs of Contini Bonacossi.

Bibliography

BARGELLINI, P., *La splendida storia di Firenze*, Florence 1964

BERTI, L., *Il principe dello Studiolo*, Florence 1967

BORSI, F., *Firenze nel Cinquecento*, Rome 1974

BUCCI, M.-BENCINI, R., *Palazzi di Firenze*, Florence 1971

CAZZATO, V.-DE VICO FALLANI, M., *Guida ai giardini urbani di Firenze*, Florence 1981

CHASTEL, A., *Art et Humanisme à Florence au temps de Laurent le Magnifique*, Paris 1959

GINORI LISCI, L., *I palazzi di Firenze nella storia e nell'arte*, Florence 1972

GOLDTHWAITE, R.A., *The Florentine Palace and Domestic Architecture*, in «American Historical Review», LXXVII, 1972

ID., *The Building of Renaissance Florence*, London 1980

LIMBURGER, W., *Die Gebäude von Florenz, Architekten, Strassen und Plätze in alphabetischen Verzeichnissen*, Leipzig 1910

MARCHINI, G., *Giuliano da Sangallo*, Florence 1943

ID., *Le finestre 'inginocchiate'*, in «Antichità Viva», I, 1976

ID., *Facciate fiorentine*, in «Antichità Viva», III, 1978

RODOLICO, F., *Le pietre delle città d'Italia*, Florence 1953, 1995[3]

ROSS, J., *Florentine Palaces and Their Stories*, London 1905

SANPAOLESI, P., *Brunelleschi*, Milan 1962

ID., *La casa fiorentina di Bartolommeo Scala*, in *Studium* zur toskanischen Kunst. Festschrift für L.H. Heydenreich, München 1964

VON STEGMANN, C.-VON GEYMÜLLER, H., *Die Architektur der Renaissance in Toskana*, München 1890-1906

THIEM, G.-THIEM, C., *Toskanische Fassadendekoration in Sgraffito und Fresko*, München 1964

TROTTA, G., *Gli antichi chiassi tra Ponte Vecchio e Santa Trinita*, Florence 1992

ZOCCHI, G., *Scelta di XXIV vedute delle principali contrade, piazze e palazzi della città di Firenze*, Florence 1744

ZUCCONI, G., *Florence. An Architectural Guide*, Venice 1995